GHOST TOWNS & MINING CAMPS
of Vancouver Island

T. W. Paterson &
Garnet Basque

GHOST TOWNS & MINING CAMPS
of Vancouver Island

IT was Sunday morning in late April, 1858, 15 years after James Douglas had landed at the southern tip of Vancouver Island to begin construction of a fort which would one day develop into the city of Victoria. In the intervening years, although sawmills, schools and roads had been built and farming had been encouraged, Fort Victoria was still a rugged, isolated Hudson's Bay Company (HBC) outpost with a population of about 300. But that was all about to change.

As the churchgoers departed Sunday services, only a few hundred yards away was a motley army of over 400, piling ashore from the ship *Commodore,* just in from San Francisco. The vanguard of a massive invasion that was about to sweep over New Caledonia, as British Columbia was then called, they had been lured north by gold — 800 ounces of which had been shipped to the San Francisco Mint aboard the HBC steamer *Otter.* With the California goldfields in decline, the news of a new goldfield had created an immediate sensation. Beginning that April, the flood continued through May, June and July. It reached its height in June, when nearly 10,000 adventurers arrived; during the first 10 days of July, 6,000 more sailed, until, it is estimated, the total number that came by land and water was between 25,000 to 30,000.

Fort Victoria was transformed overnight, as shops, stores and wooden shanties of every description sprang up everywhere. "Nothing," wrote Alfred Waddington in *The Fraser Mines Vindicated,* was to be heard but the strike of the chisel or hammer. In six weeks 225 buildings, of which nearly 200 were stores, and of these 59 belonging to jobbers or importers, had been added to a village of 800 inhabitants." Soon the country around the fort ". . .was covered with tents, resembling the encampments of an army."

Much of the population was transient, merely passing through Victoria en route to the Fraser River. Over the next five years, as they continued their northward quest for gold, newer and richer discoveries were made. In 1861, William Dietz discovered gold on Williams Creek in the Cariboo. From there the miners branched out, and virtually all streams within a 20-mile radius were found to be gold bearing. But it was not until August, 1862, when Billy Barker discovered the richest paydirt anyone had ever seen down the canyon of Williams Creek, that the Cariboo demanded everyone's attention. The town of Barkerville sprang into prominence around Barker's claim as reports of unbelievable fortunes lured men there by the hundreds.

The emergence of the Cariboo goldfields began to siphon off much of Victoria's trade and dull its importance as a major centre. To reverse this trend, Arthur Kennedy, shortly after succeeding James Douglas as governor, suggested to the citizens of Victoria that they raise subscriptions for funding an exploration party for southern Vancouver Island. With Kennedy's offer to contribute generously to the fund, the scheme was promptly acted upon. By June, 1864, the Vancouver Island Exploration Company had been formed. Led by Dr. Robert Brown, of the B.C. Botanical Society, it included Lieut. Peter J. Leech, of the Royal Engineers, artist Fred Whymper,

naturalist J. Buttle, and a staff of assistants, pioneers, miners and native hunters.

A month later, on July 14, Leech made a discovery on a tributary of Sooke River, about 25 miles from Victoria, that created great excitement. Describing the find in his despatch of July 21, Brown wrote: "The discovery with which I have to communicate is the finding of gold on the banks of one of the forks of the Sooke River, about twelve miles from the sea, in a straight line and in a locality never hitherto reached by white men, in all probability, not even by natives. I forward an eight of an ounce (or thereabouts) of the coarse scale gold washed out of twelve pans of dirt, in many places 20 feet above the river, and with no tools but a shovel and a gold pan. The lowest prospect obtained was three cents to the pan; the highest $1 to the pan, and work like that with the rocker would yield what pay you can better calculate than I can, and the development of which with what results to the colony you may imagine. The diggings extend for fully 25 miles, and would give employment to more than 4,000 men. Many of the claims would take eight to ten men to work them. The diggings could be wrought with great facility by fluming the bed of the stream. The banks and benches can be sluiced or rocked. The timber on the banks will supply to the whipsaw all the timber that can ever be required for the miner's purposes. The country abounds with game, and the 'honest miner' need never fear but that he can find food enough without much trouble. A saw mill could be erected at the head waters (or say at the forks of Leech River), and lumber for flumes, pumps, wheels, sluices, etc., floated down to the miners, and on the whole the value of the diggings cannot be easily over-estimated. I may add that there is any amount of 'five cent dirt,' and with proper tools the average prospect is about one bit to the pan. The gold will speak for itself."

During the first heady days of the rush hundreds waited at Victoria piers for news from steamers plying between the city and Sooke and excited, gesticulating men met at street corners to discuss possibilities of the strike until far into the night. The precious yellow ore exerted such tremendous drawing power upon the community that it was reported that even "the inmates of the hospital have been affected by it and several have already left for the mines."

When Capt. William Moore's steamer, the *Alexandra,* docked with the news that a $70 nugget had been found, "loud cheers of rejoicing rent the air," and the stampede was on. The miners reached the goldfield either by steamer from Victoria or by following the narrow, slippery trails over the mountains on horseback and on foot. Within weeks thousands, many of them veterans of the Fraser River gold rush of six years earlier, arrived to try their luck.

One man who made a tour through the mining district on August 14, 1864, reported that 227 mining licences had already been issued. Describing the scene, he wrote that the Dean, Thorne & Co. claim ". . .were preparing to drive a tunnel into the hill, as they had found excellent prospects, as high as 20 cents to the pan, on the top of the first bench, which is 100

(Above) Chinese washing gold in the Leech River in 1909. Note the huge boulders they had to contend with.
(Below) Most of the stores in Leechtown were of the tent variety. Here, Layzell's Retreat dispensed wines, liquors and cigars.

feet high! The claim owners stated positively that they never washed any dirt from the benches without obtaining gold. . . . They were very sanguine about getting splendid pay in the bed-rock, and believed that millions would be found in the bend of the river. On coming to the claim of the Wake-Up Jake, Mr. Fell was shown the prospect of their day's labour in a tin cup, amounting to nearly $100, and consisting of beautiful coarse gold. One company had borrowed a rickity old rocker, and had got out $25 that day, expecting to make it $40 by nightfall. Some distance above this the Balaclava Company picked up off the rocks nuggets of value varying between $5 and $10. Mr. Fell sends home very fine nuggets found without 'washing'."

During the same month, Thain & Co.'s claim was paying about two ounces of gold per day to the rocker. Another company recovered three ounces in eight hours by crevicing. Mr. Keyser, a compositor for the *Chronicle,* and his company, cleaned up $42 with a rocker in four hours, including nuggets of $7 and $4.

By this time a town of tents had sprung up on Kennedy Flat, one of which was occupied by Richard Golledge, the Gold Commissioner. Named Leechtown in honour of Peter Leech, the town soon had six general stores and three hotels open for business. During the ensuing four months it also boasted 30 saloons where miners could buy two glasses of whiskey for 25¢.

As the infant town prospered, pack trains of horses were instituted, accommodations for miners were established along the routes from Victoria, a daily four-horse coach to the junction of the Sooke trail was begun, and steamer service between the towns was increased. Initial returns from the workings justified this rapid development, the luckier miners having recovered as much as $22 worth of nuggets and coarse gold in a day's work — good wages in that halcyon age before inflation.

Satellite townships also got into the act. There was Thompson's Landing, at the mouth of the Sooke River; Kennedy, where the new government road touched the shore; and Sooke City, on the northeast slope of Sooke Harbour. Each claimed to be the best jumping-off point for the Leech River gold strike.

But not all of the adventurers and fortune hunters who flocked to the Leech and its tributaries wanted to work. This, at least, was the observation of one man, who drily noted in August, 1864: "There are about 150 people sitting about here like Micawbar (sic), waiting for something to turn up instead of trying to turn up something; they are the most orderly and lazy set of people I ever saw. They seem to fancy the gold will dig itself.

"I think if ever the river is worked it will have to be done by people of determination and industry. It will cost about $50 to the claim and one month's labor to flume and prospect the bed of the stream properly; so you see it is not a very formidable undertaking after all."

This view was confirmed by Matthew Macfie, author of *Vancouver Island and British Columbia,* which was published in 1865. "A large proportion of those who first arrived at the mines, having had no experience in the mining country, after stopping a day or two, and not finding lumps of gold visible to the naked eye, returned to Victoria discouraged, without ever striking a pick in the ground. Instances could be pointed to, where men glancing over the district superficially for a couple of days, without having brought pick, pan, shovel, or muscular power into requisition, and then retreating in a state of disappointment and indignation!"

Despite this, some work was being conducted on the Leech River during the hot summer of 1864. A shipment of $1,000 in gold dust sent to Victoria brought the total recovered to

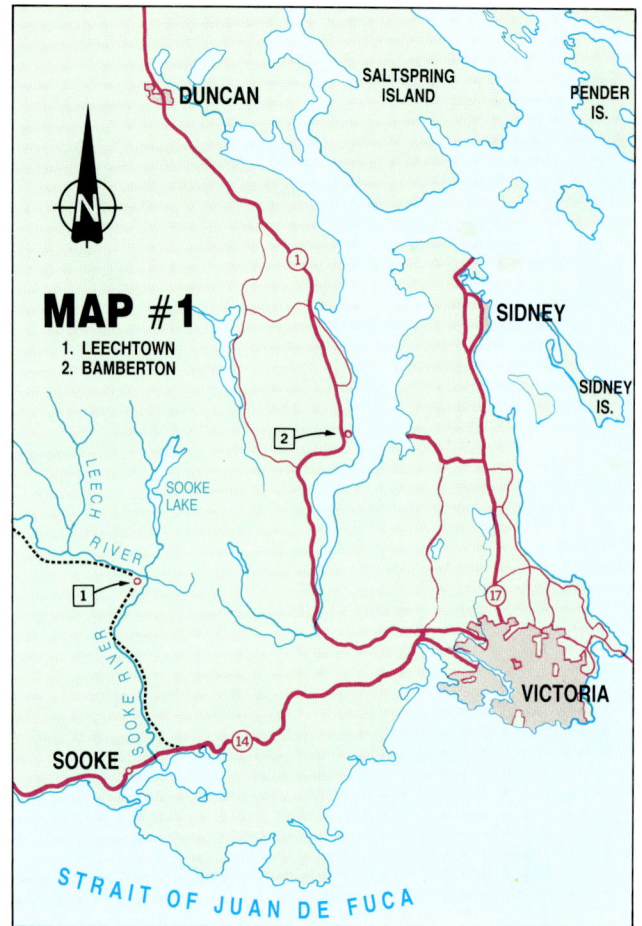

MAP #1

1. LEECHTOWN
2. BAMBERTON

DUNCAN
SALTSPRING ISLAND
PENDER IS.
SIDNEY
SIDNEY IS.
SOOKE LAKE
LEECH RIVER
SOOKE RIVER
VICTORIA
SOOKE
STRAIT OF JUAN DE FUCA

(Opposite page: The Ss Beaver off Victoria in 1846. Twelve years later this isolated HBC outpost was transformed overnight by the discovery of gold in the Fraser River.
(Below) This painting by Hind illustrates a typical prospector panning for gold in the early 1860s.

date to $1,800. An assay of the dust showed the Leech River gold, "of a rich yellow color, resembling that from Australia," to be of exceptional quality and worth $18.40 to the ounce.

Three prospectors who would have stoutly denied that no work was being done on the Leech River were Messrs. Emmick, Heal and Quick, who had invested a week of backbreaking toil trying to dig their way down to bedrock. Sinking a hole about a mile below the forks, they had battled their way through one massive boulder after another, removing the obstacles by lighting fires under them until they cracked. After a week, during which they had only penetrated 10 feet, they abandoned the pit.

Using sluiceboxes, rockers and gold pans, the miners, individually and collectively, made varied returns throughout the summer, as they sought to tap the Leech's "mother lode." But most found that, without proper equipment, they could accomplish little due to the low water level. Conversely, others complained that, despite their every effort, the river persistently flooded their claims as they attempted to dig away its banks and divert its flow. All were sure that fortunes would be made at bedrock.

A prime example of the hard work involved is provided by a description of the claims of Smith, Moffatt and Company who, at the time of a *Colonist* correspondent's visit, were "going systematically to work to reach the bedrock. Their top dirt pays tolerably well for rocking, but they have relinquished this method of mining for the present, and are now laudably endeavoring to reach the bottom of the creek by sinking a shaft, cribbing as they proceed and puddling with clay in order to keep out the water. They expect to get down 15 to 16 feet. The result of their labor will therefore be looked for with some anxiety, as the reputation of the 'Kennedy' diggings (is) in a great measure depended on."

Others were content to probe the riverbed's cracks and crevices at low water, although this was considered by most to be precarious at best.

Like all gold rushes, the Leech River stampede inspired its share of colourful names: the Last Chance, the Belfast Company, the Kangaroo Company, the Wake-Up Jake Company, the Scandinavian, the Mountain Rose. . . .

By whatever name the miners called themselves, most, according to an old veteran named Foley, shared a common handicap: inexperience. "I have seen many laboring up Leech river," he said, "asking those they met where the gold was. These men, if they had a claim, would know as much what to do with it as if they were made a present of a wild lion or an elephant!"

For Foley's money, the real strikes would be made, not in the Leech's present riverbeds, but in its banks and benches: "For to the eye of a practiced (sic) miner those banks and benches are the old bed of the river, and any man that slights them will lose thereby." Some miners heeded this advice, with what they modestly admitted to be "fine results therefrom," but the majority were amateurs who he thought would do best by rockers.

Humorous proof of his assessment was made by a ne'er-do-well and bootlegger from Victoria known as Liverpool Jack, who, upon arriving in the new diggings, proceeded to play a cruel hoax upon several other recent arrivals. When no one was looking, he salted their gold pan with 50¢ worth of dust, and the prospectors, "upon ascertaining the contents of the pan rushed back to the landing in intense excitement at the discovery." One can imagine their disappointment, and embarrassment, when the evil Liverpool Jack exposed his hoax.

For all of the miners' inexperience, it was reported that those fortunate enough to hold claims were averaging $3 a day. Most were said to be pleased with their efforts and determined to make whatever investment required to pursue the golden fleece. One of the best returns was that made by the Frederick Bar Company, who admitted to recovering "two ounces to the hand," and, according to an unconfirmed account, in one evening cleaned up 20 ounces.

As activity in the diggings intensified, camp followers, in the form of business entrepreneurs, appeared on the scene.

(Left) Lieut. Peter Leech, discoverer of gold in the Leech River. (Right) The Government House in Leechtown c1908.

A Mr. Laughlin, said to be a favourite with the miners and sure of gaining a full share of their patronage, opened a bakery and coffee shop on Kennedy Flat, at the junction of the Sooke and Leech rivers. Halfway between Victoria and the Leech, C.A. Bayley established his roadside inn — "a comfortable hotel for the accommodation of travellers" — and more and more log cabins began to appear throughout the diggings, thereby, "evidencing an intention on the part of many miners to winter on the creek."

On April 28, 1865, the *Colonist* reported that the town on Kennedy Flat had assumed ". . .the appearance of a thriving mining town, and were the streets but cleared of brush and stumps would make quite a picturesque scene. The townsite having been laid out and the streets marked, would it not be well to appropriate a couple of hundred dollars for this purpose?"

The first hotel in Leechtown was owned by H. Henley, who, in a letter dated October 25, 1864, wrote to a brother in England: "I have opened a House for whiskey and general store on the mouth of the river. I expect you will see it in the *Illustrated London News* shortly. It is named the Berks Hotel. It was the first House on the creek, 24x18 feet."

The most imposing of Leechtown's buildings was the Mount Arrarat Hotel, which was rated as a "most valuable acquisition to the mining community. It contains about a dozen rooms and the whole establishment is admirably fitted up for the comfort and convenience of its patrons." According to an advertisement in the *Colonist,* the Mount Arrarat Hotel, proprietors R.H. Johnson and R.L. Dixon, was the only hotel "fitted up" for the accommodation of ladies. "The proprietors without regard to cost or trouble have put up a House that is the admiration of all lovers of cleanliness and good eating and which would not disgrace the great metropolis of Vancouver Island."

When Governor Kennedy inspected the mines in early May, 1865, he set up his headquarters at the Arrarat. The man who had been chiefly responsible for the formation of the explora-

tion company which led to the gold discovery, was welcomed by a torchlight parade with the miners singing "For He's A Jolly Good Fellow."

For the hungry, as well as the weary, Mr. and Mrs. Rory McDonald not only offered the comforts of home in their establishment near the river junction, but "a meal prepared in the unrivalled style which has earned for Mrs. McDonald the reputation of being the best cuisiniere in the country. . . . The hotel has good accommodation for man and horse and all the delicacies of the season, including deer and bear meat."

At the goldfields themselves, some trouble had arisen over mining licences. Quoting Charles Dechant, "a practical miner," the *Colonist* noted that, "There is great dissatisfaction among the miners at the law requiring the pre-payment of the mining licence. He (Dechant) also states the parties with licences in their possession stand watching the prospectors, and when any good thing is struck, pounce on it before the actual discoverer can get it recorded."

But Leechtown's days of glory were already numbered. Almost from the beginning it had been apparent that, while the gold definitely was there — $100,000 is believed to have been taken out in that first hectic year — getting it was a horse of a different colour. For this region has been crossed more than once by glaciers which have left such a litter of boulders that reaching the gold-bearing gravels underneath is, with a few exceptions — even with today's technology — a profitless venture. Although mining interest in this region has continued unabated over the past 125 years, few major attempts have been made to wrest the Leech River gold from its long rumoured — and long-sought — mother lode.

Almost as soon as it had begun the rush was over; Leechtown had reached its peak, and passed it, by 1865. Notoriously fickle, the miners drifted away in search of new strikes in the Big Bend and elsewhere. A faithful few remained, but the town that had threatened to "empty" Victoria disintegrated into a ramshackle collection of huts. By 1874 the diggings were deserted except for an occasional visit by stray parties

The well known "Gold Pan Cabin" in happier days. Visitors have dug up the surrounding ground, poked through walls and pulled down the ceiling in their search for "treasure."

(Above) A typical miner's cabin in Leechtown in 1865.
(Left) Robert Brown was the commander of the survey party that discovered gold in Leech River.
(Opposite page, top right) Modern gold panners still try their luck near Leechtown.
(Opposite page, centre) This old car near Leechtown in 1977 is a relic of a more recent past.
(Opposite page, top left) The collapsed remains of a more recent building in Leechtown in 1977.
(Opposite page, bottom left) This vandalized cairn marks the site of the Gold Commissioner's cabin. It is constructed of rocks from the collapsed remains of the cabin's chimney. There was once a bronze plaque on the cairn explaining its significance.
(Opposite page, bottom right) This log cabin on the Mountain Rose claim was the first building on the Leech River.
(Below) The Berk's Hotel, Leechtown, 1865. Built and owned by H. Henley, it was the first commercial establishment in Leechtown.

of miners, mostly the patient Chinese.

In 1916 the B.C. *Minister of Mines* reported that a few whites and Chinese were doing some work and recovering a little gold, although it was only sufficient to provide "grub," and did not constitute standard wages. In 1928, mining engineer George Clothier examined Kennedy Flat, "sizing up the situation for dredging." He reported that "several old shafts, the deepest about 35 feet, had been sunk at different places on the flat." Although good pay had apparently been recovered from more than one of these shafts, none had ever reached bedrock. In the 1928 season several shallow pits, none over 10 feet deep, were sunk in the vicinity of the old shafts, "but no pay was found." This led Clothier to conclude that most of the gold would be found on bedrock.

In 1930 J.S. MacDonald and E. Butterworth acquired several placer leases on Leech River. The following year they installed a small hydraulic plant, "giving a head of about 200 feet in a 4-inch monitor." Several thousand yards of material were moved in cross-trenching a gravel bank, but no bedrock was encountered before low water restricted further operations.

"A winze (small incline shaft) from the bottom of the trench also failed to reach bedrock," reported Clothier in the *Minister of Mines*. "The monitor was then moved up-stream about 100 yards, where bed-rock was more evident, and this winter over 20,000 yards of gravel were moved. Rim-rock was picked up about 100 feet from the present river-bed, under about 40 feet of gravel forming the bench. The rim was followed on a gradual up-slope for over 200 feet to within 10 to 12 feet of the surface, where it turned and sloped down toward the hill, indicating an old channel. Further work proved this to be about 50 feet wide between rims, 10 feet wide on bed-rock, and about 8 feet deep above bed-rock.

"A cut was put through the rim-rock for dumping into the present river and a cut put across the old channel, which gave promising returns of fairly coarse gold. The cut through the rim will have to be deepened, the sluice brought through or grade to bed-rock, and a considerable yardage of the old channel washed through before any definite idea can be found of the importance of the find. It certainly looks promising."

In 1931, Clothier reported that efforts made by three or four parties to find placer diggings on Leech River had been largely unsuccessful. As for MacDonald and Butterworth, they had improved their water supply by diverting Humbug Creek into MacDonald Lake by a ditch and raising a dam at the lower end. There operations must not have proved worthwhile, however, as there is no further mention of it.

Of Leechtown itself, never more than shanties, nothing has survived subsequent mining activities and, more recently, logging operations. About a mile from Leechtown, on Wolf Creek, some evidence remains of the old Eagle Talc and Mining Company's property — one of the very few operations in this region which was not in search of gold. But, aside from the ruins described, and those in the area which date back only as far as large-scale logging, visitors will have to contend themselves with what few clues to the past they can find along the river banks and in the trees.

Not surprisingly, the recent upsurge in the price of gold has reawakened interest in Leech River and its tributaries. But despite many attempts, some of them fairly substantial, no one has succeeded in striking it rich. According to one late prospector, who managed to raise a family during the Depression on the gold he recovered in the area, there are no "pay-streaks. One has to have determination and lots of luck to have much success there."

Statistics in the provincial department of mines show that, between the years of 1921-45, only 192 ounces of gold, worth $5,807, was taken from Leech River. Best returns were made on the west and south forks of the river, the north fork having yielded little more than colour.

But Leechtown's ability to arouse the imagination has not paled during the past century. Even today men search for a reputedly lost treasure. The story, involving $40,000 in gold dust which was supposedly buried by Rattlesnake Dick Barter, an American highwayman, has often been told — most writers and treasure hunters blissfully ignoring the fact that the gold never left California.[1]

Little more than a scenic hour's drive from downtown Victoria, the site of Leechtown is easy to trace, despite the fact that excessive logging operations have totally changed the countryside. Unfortunately, modern-day visitors will find little evidence of the Leech River's past glory. The historic townsite is gone, overgrown by fir and alder on the river bank. Only a vandalized cairn, constructed in 1928 using rocks from the old Gold Commissioner's cabin, lies almost hidden in the undergrowth. Originally it bore the inscription: "Memorial erected by B.C. Historical Association on site of gold commissioner's house to commemorate discovery of gold on Sooke river by Lieut. P.J. Leech, July 1864, and to mark the site of Leechtown which sprang up following discovery." On either side are the gnarled remains of two apple trees planted by Governor Kennedy's daughter in 1864.

A second smaller plaque informed visitors that "All historic objects in this vicinity have been placed under protection of the Historic Objects Preservation Art of B.C. and any interference is subject to penalty."

A hundred feet or so down the road, to the left, a small clearing contains a tumble-down cabin and the remains of several shacks and a water tower. These, however, are not the original town, although fairly old. The dilapidated condition of the cabin, identified by a plaque as an "historic gold miner's cabin," is not completely the result of age and weather; vandals and "treasure hunters" have dug up the surrounding ground, poked through wallboard and pulled down ceilings in their search for treasure. Hundreds of small holes in the rotting timber are not evidence of woodpeckers, either, but the handiwork of hunters who have used the cabin for target practice.

Such depredations have, in the past, resulted in the entire area (which is privately owned) being closed to the public. A disgusted logging official explained several years ago: "They were taking everything that would move."

Visitors to the area today will find it difficult to imagine that, 125 years ago, Leechtown and neighbouring Boulder City consisted of no fewer than 1,200 mines and, reputedly, at one time attracted as many as 4,000 adventurers. But, although some collapsed cabins and abandoned mining equipment are to be found throughout the region, of the town's original stores, "hotels" (none of them more than glorified log shanties), saloons and gold commissioner's office (perhaps the only substantial structure Leechtown had ever known), nothing but the battered cairn remains.

Because the original claims were reworked during the Depression, much of the old machinery one finds rusting under the carpeting of moss is of comparatively recent vintage. ♣

[1]For the full story about this lost treasure, see *Lost Bonanzas of Western Canada*, Sunfire Publications, 1988.

Bamberton

B.C. Cement Company's Plant at Bamberton in 1925.

THE tens of thousands of motorists who annually use the scenic Malahat drive likely do not remember the dusty shroud that for so long cloaked the trees and guardrails of this southern stretch of the Island Highway.

Today historic Bamberton, for almost three-quarters of a century a leading producer of Portland cement, is no more. With its passing, the dust problem which had enveloped much of the highway between Goldstream and Mill Bay solved itself. Once again the trees are green; sadly, this boon to the environment has been achieved at the expense of nearly 200 jobs. . . .

Actually, the cement works at Bamberton had its start on the opposite side of Saanich Inlet, in smaller Tod Inlet, in 1904 when the Vancouver Portland Cement Company established a large cement manufacturing plant. President of the company was E.R. Woods, of Toronto while R.P. Butchart was the managing director. Butchart had held the same position with allied cement companies at Shallow Lake and Lakefield in Ontario. Today, a 260-foot-high smokestack stands as silent monument to the original quarrying and cement plant, but, in its day, the company played an active role in the economic health of southern Vancouver Island.

Although the Tod Inlet plant was connected to Victoria, 13 miles distant, by a wagon road, and was only 2½ from Keating, a station on the Victoria & Sidney Railway, all of its product was shipped by water. The factory buildings were about 100 feet from the shore of the inlet, into which a substantial pile wharf, about 36 feet wide, had been run for about 200 feet. This wharf was arranged to receive two scows on either side, while the end was provided with an adjustable apron to connect with car-transfer scows, from which the railway cars could be run directly into the works to be loaded or unloaded, standard gauge tracks having been laid for this purpose.

The five factory buildings were arranged in such a way as to practically form one; in some instances the dividing walls consisted of pillars only. The walls of all the buildings were of concrete about 15 inches thick and 20 feet high. The roof trusses were made of wood, with iron tension bolts, while the

roofs were boards covered with malthoid, a prepared roofing felt. Because the manufacturing of cement created so much dust, the cement walls were surmounted by a wooden framework about eight feet high, filled in with wooden lattice work.

For the sake of compactness, the working floors of the plant were all on the same level, the material being elevated by mechanical means between the successive stages. The exception was the stockroom which was 10 feet lower than the factory floors.

A description of the process followed by the Tod Inlet plant, and later, the Bamberton plant, in the manufacture of cement, is certainly worth describing. All of the material required, namely limestone and clay, was mined at the site. The quarries were connected to the preliminary crushing plant by a tramline, which carried the raw materials into the end of the building at the eve level and deposited it into large limestone or clay storage bins.

Located just under the floor level of these bins was the feed end of a Gates crusher, into which the limestone was deposited. The crushed limestone was then discharged into a "rotary dryer," a hollow wrought iron cylindrical shell five feet in diameter and 42 feet long. As the cylinder revolved, the crushed limestone travelled through the dryer which was heated by waste gasses from the "rotary kiln."

The crushed and thoroughly dried limestone was then discharged into a screw conveyor, which carried it horizontally, underneath the floor level, to the boot of a bucket-elevator. The material was then raised and deposited in the feed bin of a "Krupp ball mill," a horizontally-revolving iron shell, about six feet in diameter and six feet long. The mill was lined with a heavy, chilled-iron screen and contained a number of round, steel balls. As the mill revolved, these balls rolled over and through the partially crushed limestone, gradually grinding it until it was fine enough to pass through the enclosing 100 mesh screen. The finely ground limestone was then discharged through the end of the cylinder directly into a bucket-elevator, by which it was raised and deposited in the "ground limestone

(Above & below) *The Vancouver Portland Cement Company's works at Tod Inlet. The top photo was taken in 1903, while the lower one was taken in 1911.*
(Opposite page) *The site of the Tod Inlet cement works is now the world famous Butchart Gardens.*

stock-bin." The bottom of this bin, which had a storage capacity of about 50 tons, was some eight feet above floor level.

Delivered over the same tramway as the limestone, the clay was dumped into a "Potts disintegrator," a pair of rollers and revolving knife-like teeth which thoroughly disintegrated it. From here it passed through the dryer which was used, as required, alternately for limestone or clay. Leaving the dryer, the clay was so finely ground it did not need to pass through the Krupp ball mill, and was elevated directly to the "ground clay stock-bin," a companion bin to that in which the ground limestone was stored. At this point the materials, which so far in the process have been treated and handled separately, were mixed.

In front of each of these bins was an automatic weighing scale, so constructed that it could be set to receive a definite weight of ground material. By adjusting these two scales any desired weight of limestone or clay could be weighed off and gradually discharged from both scale hoppers into one horizontally placed screw conveyor, in which the two ingredients were thoroughly mixed. This mixture was then conveyed to an elevator, raised, then deposited in an elevated hopper bin. From here gravity fed the mixture down into two "tube mills," in which it was still more fully incorporated and ground.

These tube mills, as the names implies, were iron tubes made of boiler plate, about five feet in diameter and 22 feet long. Set horizontally on rollers, they revolved about 25 times a minute. These tubes were lined with very hard, tough, cut flint stones, imbedded in cement, the lining having a thickness of several inches. Inside the mill, and loose, were a number of larger, round flint pebbles, which rolled over and through the ground limestone and clay, fully mixing and more finely grinding them. This thoroughly ground and mixed material was then discharged from the lower end of the tube mills into a common screw conveyor. It was then carried to another elevator, raised, then deposited by gravity into the "rotary kiln."

Lined with firebrick, the rotary kiln was an iron tube, seven feet in diameter and 70 feet long. As the cylinder, which was mounted on rollers at a slight incline, revolved, it gradually carried the material from its upper end to its lower end. There it was discharged through a chute into the boot of an elevator. The interior of the kiln was maintained at a temperature of about 2,700 degrees Fahrenheit by the combustion of fine, dry coal dust, so fine as to act as a gas, which was fed into the cylinder by a blast of air.

The particles of the finely crushed limestone and clay fed into the upper end of the kiln were, in their slow passage through this fiery furnace, sintered or fused together. This formed what is known as "cement clinker." The red-hot clinker discharged from the kiln was raised by an open link-belt bucket-elevator to the level of the walls of the building and shot down a wrought iron tube to the "rotary cooler," which was a revolving iron cylinder about five feet in diameter and 50 feet long, through which a draft of cool air was induced. This so cooled the clinker that it came out of the lower end at a temperature sufficiently reduced to permit its further handling. As the cooled clinker dropped from the cooler, any large pieces were automatically screened out and broken by hand.

This clinker, when pulverized, is cement. However, if water was added it would instantly set hard as granite. To avoid this "flash setting," about one per cent gypsum was added to retard the setting stage. At first the gypsum was imported

from the central western states, as none was as yet being mined in the province.

From the cooler the clinker dropped into an elevator and was deposited in an elevated hopper bin, from which it was automatically fed into a "Bonnot" ball mill, five feet in diameter and eight feet long. This mill, similar to the Krupp mill, partially crushed the clinker. From the Bonnot mill the material was conveyed by a screw conveyor to an elevator and discharged into another tube mill, which pulverized the finished cement finer than 100-mesh. It was then carried by a conveyor belt to the stock room, where it was deposited in bins ready for sacking and subsequent shipment. Each sack held 87½ pounds, and it took four sacks to make a barrel.

The powerhouse was a building separate from, but adjoining, the factory, with concrete walls and partitions separating the engine and boiler rooms. Steam was generated in a battery of five tubular boilers, fired partly by wood and partly by coal. The engine was a 600-hp compound Corliss, and was supplied with condenser, pumps, feed water heater, etc. While power was first generated by steam, it was the intention of the company to operate eventually by electric power.

Adjoining the engine and boiler-house was a separate building, about 50 feet by 80 feet. This "coal grinding plant" was where the fuel for the rotary kiln was prepared. About half of the building consisted of coal storage bins, which were connected by a belt conveyor directly to a scow alongside the wharf. From these bins the coal was taken by a link elevator to a Bartlett rotary cylindrical dryer — essentially an inclined, revolving, iron cylinder, about five feet in diameter and 20 feet long — heated externally underneath by a firebox using both wood and coal. In its passage through the heated cylinder the coal was thoroughly dried, then conveyed to a Raymond three-roll mill, which crushed the coal until it was fine enough to be carried to an elevated iron tank in the kiln building, from which it was fed as required into the kiln by a blast of air.

The Tod Inlet plant had a capacity of 300 barrels of Portland cement a day. However, with increased machinery, for which accommodation had already been provided in the present buildings, the capacity could be doubled on short notice. In April, 1905, the first shipment of cement was made by the barge *Alexander*. In 1907 the plant at Tod Inlet made and sold nearly 150,000 barrels of Portland cement (350 pounds to the barrel), worth nearly $225,000. This was more than its capacity of only two years earlier. Of this quantity, 125,000 barrels were used in British Columbia.

Four year later the *B.C. Mining Record* reported that the Vancouver Portland Cement Company "intends electrifying its plant and has contracted with the B.C. Electric Railway Company to supply 500-hp from its new Jordan River plant as soon as ready, the company proposes ultimately to increase the service by another 2,500-hp.

"For temporary service the Vancouver Portland Cement Works recently purchased from the Allis-Chalmers-Bullock Company a 500-hp turbo-generator. The steam plant hitherto in use will be retained in case of accident to the electric service."

To drive the various sections of the plant the company purchased 42 electric motors from Canadian General Electric. The report concluded by stating that production had been increased from 1,100 barrels a day to 2,000. It also pointed out several new additions to the plant: "a new kiln room, transformer room, drying room 205 feet by 40 feet; two new kilns with reinforced concrete stack 175 feet in height. A dust collecting chamber will also be added to the plant to collect the dust from the works and prevent the smothering of the vegetation surrounding the works as hitherto."

The years spanning the turn of the century witnessed one of the greatest economic booms in provincial history, and Butchart intended to fill the construction industry's need for cement. When production at Tod Inlet outstripped the quarry's capability, Butchart cast his eyes across Saanich Inlet. At the foot of the Malahat was an area that promised a greater yield of limestone, and it was here that a second plant was constructed. The new Bamberton plant commenced production in 1912.

In 1914 the *Minister of Mines* reported that two companies manufactured cement in the province during the year. "The Vancouver Portland Cement Company, with works at Tod Inlet, is said to have produced 360,000 barrels worth $560,000. The Associated Cement Company, with works at Bamberton, made a production valued at about $300,000." Both operations were operated by the B.C. Cement Company Ltd., of Victoria.

In 1915 the Tod Inlet plant produced about 120,000 barrels of Portland cement, valued at approximately $200,000. This output was only about a quarter of that of 1912, but was probably all the market could absorb because "of the depression in the building trades." The Bamberton plant had greater success, producing about 156,000 barrels worth about $265,000.

During the same year the Bamberton plant installed a Bucyrus 25B revolving type electric shovel. Built by the Bucyrus Co. of South Milwaukee, Wisconsin, the 32-ton shovel arrived in Victoria on May 2 aboard the Ss *Buenaventura* via the Panama Canal. Transferred to Bamberton, it was erected and put into service on May 15.

The following year the Bamberton plant only produced about 90,000 barrels of cement worth about $156,000. It was an ominous warning to what lay ahead, for, with the outbreak of the First World War, the real estate boom crashed and all but eliminated construction projects and the demand for cement. For nearly seven years both plants sat idle. However, with the return of peacetime, Bamberton slowly resumed production in 1921. Three years later the plant employed 180 men and produced upwards of a million dollars in cement. By this time, cement was being manufactured by the "wet method."

The limestone was put through a crusher. Instead of clay, shale was added in the proportion of one to three. This compound was then ground to powder and 30 to 32 per cent water added, giving the material the appearance of thick white soup. This "slurry" was then pumped to slurry mixers, huge open concrete tanks 66 feet in diameter and eight feet deep. Here it was thoroughly mixed by revolving paddles set under the revolving platform. While the mixture was in these pools it was chemically tested and adjustments were made, if necessary, to bring it up to standard quality.

From these pools the slurry was pumped to the kilns, which were 185 feet long and nine feet in diameter. Set on an incline and revolving, they were lined with firebrick and heated by pulverized coal to a temperature of 2,700 degrees. Entering at the head of these, the slurry took three hours to work its way through, emerging at the far end thoroughly dry, and looking like black peas. It was then cooled in revolving coolers and ground to a fineness that permitted it to pass through a screen of 10,000 apertures per square inch. This screen was so unbelievably fine that it could actually hold water!

After this the gypsum was added and the cement stored in one of 28 cement storage bins, each with a capacity of 2,600 barrels. From there it was shipped to market, as required, in the company's three boats, the *Island King, Shean* or *Teco,* carrying 16,000, 10,000 or 6,500 sacks each.

R.P. Butchart, president of the B.C. Cement Company, was one of the best known and most public-spirited men in the province. The abandoned pit at Tod Inlet was developed by him and his wife into the famous "Sunken Gardens," transforming an eyesore into a spot of marvellous beauty. These gardens he threw open to the public and they were greatly enjoyed by Victorians and visitors to that city. Today, we know them as the world famous Butchart Gardens.

By 1927 the Bamberton plant had reached a capacity of 3,000 barrels per day and was contributing $700,000 annually to the local economy in the form of salaries and supplies. The plant used 40,000 tons of Vancouver Island coal each year, it taking 130 pounds to burn one barrel of cement. Because of its isolation, Bamberton, like many a mining and lumber settlement before it, became a self-contained community, complete with blacksmith shop, general stores and even a townsite. Most supplies were brought in by company tug and barge in the years before the deer trail over the Malahat became a modern highway.

During its peak the Bamberton plant employed about 180 men, all of whom resided on the company's property. The main village sat on a shelf in the mountain-side above the quarries, but additional quarters were located near the shore. The company made every effort to keep its employees cheerful and contented. In a huge recreation hall, with a dancing floor just as large as that of the Empress Hotel, and every bit as smooth, gay parties were staged every week.

The Island Highway proved to be a further blessing in that it allowed the company to haul limestone by truck from the Cobble Hill-Shawnigan Lake district when the original Bamberton quarries began to play out. This was but a reprieve, however, and Bamberton's career as a producer of Portland cement steadily declined during the last 20 years. A bitter, protracted strike, increased production costs, and ever-changing markets spelled *finis* for the Malahat mill town in the 1980s.

In October, 1982, Bamberton became the latest of a long line of Vancouver Island ghost towns when the following advertisement appeared in a Duncan newspaper: "For Sale: 2,000 acres of choice southern Vancouver Island property, with three miles of waterfront, including sandy beaches, deep water wharf, and heritage-style cement plant. Asking price $13 million."

The "heritage-style" cement works, then owned by Genstar, the multinational conglomerate, formed the nucleus of one of the largest private real estate holdings on Vancouver Island; upon eventual sale it would rival Robert Dunsmuir's Esquimalt & Nanaimo Railway grant. But for the old plant and homes, much of the property remains in its natural state — a realtor's dream, as it even has its own waterworks. Within a half-hour's drive of Victoria and Duncan, Bamberton seems fated to become a bedroom satellite of both the capital city and its northern neighbour. Only the price tag seems to have deterred development along this line to date.

(For a time Toyota Canada played with the idea of establishing an automotive plant here, but decided against it because of the need to reship everything to the mainland.) Other foreign firms have looked at the property, a German syndicate having expressed interest in converting the mill site into a

$50 million hotel-condominium-marina complex. The provincial government also has considered the possibility of acquiring a 100-acre parcel adjacent to Bamberton Park (originally part of the cement property).

Demolition of the mill began late in 1982, but Bamberton's career as a cement plant will long be recalled by its quarries (it is highly unlikely that the Butchart Gardens miracle will be repeated here) and the whitish patina which glazes all rock outcroppings from the beach to the summit of the Malahat — the residue of decades of concrete, formed of rain and the lime dust which for so long has enveloped the mountain-side.

As late as October 1982, there was a modern-day ghost town, overgrown by vegetation and invisible to passers-by on the highway above. Situated at the end of an access road (constructed of concrete, of course) from the highway, this was Bamberton village. Although of earlier vintage, these homes had been well built and some were yet worth salvaging. Almost inevitably, windows had been broken by vandals, the cement-stucco houses were cloaked by brambles, sidewalks were cracked and spired with weeds, and once neatly trimmed hedges had gone wild.

Most houses have since been demolished, although some were transported to new locations. Buyers had been attracted by advertisements such as this one, which appeared in a January 1983 edition of the Cowichan *News: "Bamberton Home.* Must be moved right away. 1000 sq. ft. wood floors throughout. Excellent opportunity to get a beautiful, instant home on your property at a very reasonable price...."

One of the last survivors of Bamberton was, curiously, its single brick building. Inscribed "Bamberton Cement Works, 1912," it recalled Bamberton's heyday as a cement plant — and served as a stark reminder that, even in the '80s, once thriving communities can become ghost towns. ♣

(Top & bottom right) The site of the Bamberton cement works is now a British Columbia provincial park.
(Below) The first automobile in Bamberton, 1912.

Mount Sicker

MILLIONS in sight. . .a nearby treasure house in Mount Sicker! Such was the golden prophecy made in the spring of 1897 for the newly-discovered copper deposits on Mount Sicker, 50 miles north of Victoria. Within four years, two major mines, a railway, and not one, but three new townsites were to bloom on the steep bluffs of previously unheralded, 2,300-foot Mount Sicker.

The saga began in the fall of 1895 when three American prospectors named Sullins, McKay and Buzzard, discovered promising tracings of copper, silver and gold on Mount Sicker and staked the Alice, Leona, Belle and Gold Queen claims. However, as it was late in the season work on a mine-shaft on the Leona claim was suspended for the winter and the three returned to Port Townsend. With spring, Sullins, Buzzard, and a new partner, Harry Smith (McKay having died) returned to Mount Sicker.

Briefly stimulated when one of Smith's relatives put up $500 for a half-interest in three of the properties (including the latest, the Little Nugget), the partners went to work with renewed energy. But the money soon ran out, their latest partner returned to the Old Country in disgust, and Sullens, Buzzard and Smith were on their own once more. For a year, they did their best with limited resources, faithfully prospecting the surrounding mountain-side and continuing to push their shaft on the Leona claim.

Nature intervened in August, 1896, when a devastating forest fire swept the western face of Mount Sicker. So fierce was this fire that the smoke clouds veiled the sun for days and the ashes were carried by the wind for miles over the surrounding country. The miners fled for their lives, but their cabin and effects were consumed by the flames. Ironically, the fire proved to be a blessing in disguise. The following spring Harry Smith, acting on his own, found a 30-foot-wide outcropping of copper at the 1,400-foot level that had been revealed by the fire. Smith named the new strike Lenora, after his daughter. Shortly after, with Henry Buzzard, he staked a second claim, the Tyee.

For years, Cowichan Valley settlers had dreamed of such a strike: Something concrete in the way of industry which would act as a stabilizer for their purely agricultural economy. When word of the strike on nearby Mount Sicker was made public, the rush was on. Scores of hopeful prospectors downed ploughshares and pitchforks to take to the slopes of Mount Sicker and neighbouring hills in search of fame and fortune. Within weeks the little mountain was staked and counterstaked with more than 60 claims.

When, in June, a successful prospector (possibly one of the original partners, Buzzard) passed through Victoria, residents were ecstatic at his news. Reported the *Colonist:* "A small piece of almost solid mineral, running in value, according to assays, $6 in silver, $14 in gold and about $17 in copper, was exhibited by a prospector on the Hudson's Bay wharf last evening, just before his departure for the Sound. The quartz came from a claim not 50 miles away, situated on Mount Sicker, which mountain is now staked from base to summit,

according to the testimony of the bearer of the specimen.

"Mount Sicker faces the (Esquimalt & Nanaimo) Railway at Westholme, and extends for some five miles in the direction of Chemainus River. The particular claim from which the well-mineralized specimen comes is the Le Nora (sic), a property located one year ago, when a horse trail was built to it and something like $1,000 worth of development work done. This year a new lead has been discovered, which promises to be a fortune to the finder.

"This lead is almost 30 feet in width and extends on the surface for 40 feet, at an elevation of 50 feet for every hundred, working up the slope of the mountain side. A break in the formation exposes a 60-foot facing of the ore body, and a tunnel could be drifted in at the lowest level and the ore literally quarried out — making it a shipping proposition from the 'grassroots down,' to adopt the prospector's phraseology.

"Figuring the ore body at 400 feet in length, 200 feet down, and 15 feet wide (this being only half the exposed width), there is about $5,000,000 worth of ore in sight. . . ."

The only fly in the ointment, as noted by the Victoria newspaper, was the lack of a road to the mines, although it was assured that "this would not involve any great expense in construction." The fact that the rich claims on Mount Sicker were so near the Esquimalt & Nanaimo Railway (E&N), and that far again from tidewater, seemed to guarantee the new mine of a rosy future, and "the settlers and prospectors in the district are naturally very desirous that the road should be taken in hand by the government without delay."

Already, three mining camps were beginning to make an appearance in the wilderness, as up to 30 men laboured at "full blast sinking on prospects from which assays as high as $32 have been obtained." On the Leona claim, a shaft had reached a depth of 22 feet; two 15-foot test holes had been driven on the Belle; two 12-footers at the Alice; one 16-footer at the Pioneer, and, at the Golden Queen, "People have gone down 18 feet."

So enthusiastic were the principals behind the Lenora, that the unnamed prospector informed the *Colonist:* "The day is not far distant when a smelter will be erected either on the property or conveniently located."

This had been a fervent dream of many British Columbians: Canadian smelters for Canadian ore!

Smith, discoverer of the Lenora, wasted no time in promoting the Lenora, Mount Sicker and British Columbia Development Company, and work on a tunnel into the mountain was pushed at all possible speed. Mining was considered economical in Mount Sicker's schist belt, with 5-foot by 7-foot tunnels costing only $4.50 a foot, and within a year the main shaft was 500 feet long. Then, it seems, the company again ran short of funds. It was the age-old curse of mining, with every new step requiring new money. This time, however, they attracted the attention of influential investors — and the Lenora, Mount Sicker Copper Mining Company was formed under the direction of Henry Croft, an in-law of the powerful James Dunsmuir of coal mining fame.

Under Croft's personal and expert direction, work was stepped up, and a miniature townsite was surveyed to the northwest of the mine. Before long homes, a school, general store and livery stable appeared amid the silent firs and cedars crowning Mount Sicker. By 1900 the Lenora was connected with Westholme and Duncan by wagon roads of seven and nine miles, respectively, and boasted daily stage service with the railway station at Westholme.

As an expression of confidence in its development, the company advertised a sale of lots: "Mount Sicker Townsite. The future Rossland of Vancouver Island. The Mount Sicker Company have decided to place their townsite on the market for sale. For the next 30 days we will sell corner lots at $75, and inside lots at $50. Terms: one third cash, one third in three months, one third in six months, and to the first 10 purchasers who will erect buildings on their lots, we will make a reduction of 50 per cent in price of lots. The townsite adjoins the Lenora mine which is shipping 60 tons of ore daily. This is a chance for investment, and not to be missed."

Not only had the Lenora entered production in this period, but, by the beginning of 1900, it had become the fourth largest shipper of copper ore in the province. By this time the sawmill that had been erected served as the means of starting the townsite upon which some 18 houses had already been built. A hotel was also under construction which, it was expected, would "be a boon to the district."

Several factors had contributed to this rapid rate of development. Firstly, upon completion of the wagon road, the mines at Mount Sicker enjoyed full connection with the E&N, and, through its services, the rest of the Pacific Northwest. Also, the availability of the ore, its exceptionally high grade, and a ready water supply meant almost immediate returns of the sizable investment made to date. To March 23, 1901, the Lenora had shipped 11,867 tons of ore valued at $175,831. From March 23 to May 6 of the same year an additional 2,276 tons had been shipped.

Ironically, the Lenora quickly realized that success could be a problem in itself when production began to outpace the roadway's capability to haul the washed and bagged ore "outside" by horse-team. To overcome this problem a tram track was laid from Westholme Station to within three miles of the mine during the spring of 1900. Utilizing the new tramway, shipments were increased to about 30 tons a day.

During the summer of 1900, after the tramway system became overtaxed, plans were made for construction of a railway. Operated by a Shay-geared locomotive and self-dumping cars of 15 tons capacity each, the narrow-gauge Lenora, Mount Sicker Railway (LMS), built at a cost of about $45,000, was to make railway history for Vancouver Island. Although only six miles long at first, the LMS has been described as being one of the most difficult and dangerous trackways ever laid in the province. Engineers faced a nightmare of 50-degree curves, switchbacks and trestles along the face of sheer cliffs, and a grade so steep that it resembled a roller coaster ride.

After completion of the railway the Lenora mine was at last able to fulfil its commitments to a Tacoma smelter. This, despite the fact that its railroad navigated such hairpin curves that it became a matter of local lore that the trains often spilled much of their cargoes from the open ore cars when roaring down the mountain-side at breakneck speed. The descent was so rapid that brakemen had to ride on each ore car — each at the ready to apply the brakes should the locomotive gain too much headway. As an added precaution, the

steeper grades were sanded before each descent. Passengers unused to such travel claimed that they were compelled to "sit on the side of this oscillating vehicle with their feet dangling over the precipice!" Despite such terrifying hazards the *Colonist* urged its readers to brave the ride on the side of an ore car and view the spectacular scenery to be enjoyed at the little town in the wilderness, which, according to the *B.C. Mining Record,* gave every indication it was "building up into a permanent, prosperous and progressive town."

As the Lenora continued to produce and the railway managed to keep up with its output, Croft decided to take his operation one step further by building his own smelter at nearby Osborn Bay. There, at tidewater, another community was born and named Crofton after its founder. At the peak of production some 400 men were employed here. Ironically, although the Lenora has long gone the way of most pioneer mines, Crofton survives as a large mill and shipping port for Vancouver Island lumber products.

Throughout this busy period for Henry Croft and company, others had been hard at work at exploiting the copper, silver, and gold treasure of Mount Sicker. A Vancouver company owned the Queen Bee property, a California interest the Key City claim, the Mount Sicker and British Columbia Development Company was hard at work on its Seattle group of claims, and Mounts Sicker and Brenton Mines Limited, to the west in Copper Canyon, was aglow after having driven a hundred-foot shaft through a high-paying ore body.

The Lenora's toughest competition was to come from a well-heeled English syndicate, the Tyee Copper Company, which was born in London in April 1900, with substantial finances, and on July 1 assumed control of the floundering Tyee Development Company. Prior to that time a shaft had been sunk to a depth of 200 feet with crosscuts north and south from the 160-foot level. A year later, the new firm, which now owned Harry Smith's interest in the Tyee claim, as well as a continuous chain of claims as far as the Chemainus River, had its own mine, sawmill and townsite. During the previous winter equipment consisting of two 50-hp boilers, a hoisting engine and a three drill air compressor had been installed.

"Renewed activity is already taking place in mining on Mt. Sicker," reported the Duncan *Weekly Enterprise* (whose publisher was none other than Harry Smith, former prospector). "The Tyee mine is actively developing under the management of Messrs. Claremont (sic) Livingston, Pellew-Harvey and E. Musgrave, resident engineer. The machinery for the mine is now on the way, and as soon as it arrives a large force of men will be employed. Development will be carried on to fully prove the property before ore shipping is undertaken."

A week later Smith, who understandably took a proprietary interest in mining affairs on Mount Sicker, informed his readers that the Tyee Company was "getting things in good shape to carry on large workings, additional quarters being added. A new store-room is to be built at once and by the time the machinery arrives they will be all ready to put it in place. The Tyee will be the first mine on Mt. Sicker to operate with machinery."

In London a stockholders' meeting had been held, directors of the firm proudly informing their audience that the first issue of shares had been sold out in little more than a month. Although a "tropical state of weather" was blamed for having reduced attendance, the board chairman was happy to inform those present that, according to Clermont Livingston, resident manager of the mine: "...The prospects look brighter than

(Above) Clermont Livingston, General Manager of the Tyee Copper Co. Ltd. in 1904.

(Right) No. 1, first of four locomotives used on the Lenora, Mount Sicker Railway. Due to its ingenious system of switchbacks it has been described as one of the most difficult and dangerous trackways in B.C. history. Some of the grades were so steep and the curves so sharp, that brakemen had to ride on each and every car so as to be able to apply the brakes at a moment's notice.

(Below left) Exploratory development work at the Lenora mine.

(Below right) Lenora's famous No. 1 mine. Today, several ore cars such as that shown in the photograph are to be found abandoned on the silent, tree-covered slopes of Mount Sicker.

(Above) The new bunkers and sorting shed at the Lenora mine in 1901.
(Below) The terminus of the Lenora mine in 1901.

ever (and) the developments on the adjoining claims show that we are on the top of an immense body of good ore. If further evidence were required through our whole property it is found in the rich yellow copper ore which has been struck on the 'Magic Fraction,' while on the west, in the 'Lenora' claim, they are shipping very rich ore at the rate of about 50 tons a day."

Situated several hundred feet above the Lenora townsite, the Tyee camp boosted the population of Mount Sicker to almost 2,000 persons and made its combined population the fourth largest on the Island.

Upon completion of a new wagon road from Mount Prevost, and the establishment of a regular coach and mail service, those working at the mines no longer felt quite so isolated. As competitors the townsites of Lenora and Tyee vied for supremacy. When Tyee got its post office, Lenora demanded its own. With the building of the luxurious, 18-room Mount Sicker Hotel and a 40-pupil schoolhouse, Lenora was able to snub its younger neighbour and pass itself off to the world as the future Rossland of Vancouver Island. Then Tyee responded with its own posh hostelry, the Brenton Hotel, and went Lenora one better with a church. Finally, the owners of the latter mine (more for reasons of business than for rivalry) established twice-daily passenger service between the town and the E&N at Westholme, and extended the LMS to the smelter at Crofton. This oneupmanship was to have fatal consequences for both communities.

For Henry Croft this final link in his little railroad was a godsend, as, previously, the Lenora had been limited to shipment of only its high grade ore due to the costs involved. With his own railway line right to the company smelter, Croft was able to utilize a large stockpile of second grade ore, and the company began to show a handsome profit.

In the autumn of 1901, after two and a half years of steady development, the Tyee directors began considering the most economical method of shipping and treating their ore. A further £50,000 was subscribed which raised the company's capital to £180,000 in 180,000 shares at £1 each. A contract was awarded to B.C. Riblet of Nelson to construct an automatic aerial tram on the double rope system, to connect the mines with the E&N. The length of the tram, which had a maximum capacity of 400 tons per day, was three and a half miles.

The Tyee company's development of its two miles of underground workings proceeded steadily and, by the spring of 1903, it too boasted its own smelter. Situated to the west of the town of Ladysmith, the smelter lay between the E&N tracks and Oyster Bay with approximately 3,000 feet of waterfront. The plant had a capacity of 200 tons per day, but the powerhouse, smelting shed and dust chamber were built to accommodate a capacity of 600 tons, only additional equipment being required.

The ore was conveyed from the Tyee mine in bottom dumping cars of the E&N, which delivered it into two sets of bins at the roast yard, each with a capacity of 1,600 tons. From there the ore was trammed out over a series of six permanent trestles placed 60 feet apart and running north and south. The smelter building was 81 feet in length by 51 feet wide. The engine and boiler house on the east of the smelter shed and 60 feet distant, was 70 feet by 50 feet. In the rear of the boiler was a 20 foot by 20 foot coal bunker over which a spur from the E&N track ran for the delivery of coal for power purposes.

By 1903 the Tyee had shipped 42,000 tons of ore worth almost $600,000. This had not been achieved without cost and effort, however, as, like the Lenora, the Tyee had been plagued by the expense of shipping its ore from isolated Mount Sicker. At first it tried the old method of horse and wagon, with the same negative results as its competitor down the hill. As its ore dumps continued to build up faster than they could be transported to the E&N siding at Somenos, the company turned its attention to an aerial tramway, a system of cables and buckets which, when completed late in 1902, was almost as ingenious and death-defying as the LMS. In less than four miles, the loaded bucket of ore dropped 1,900 feet to the E&N siding. At peak of production it handled 5,000 tons of ore a month and was said to be the longest single section

The Tyee Co.'s hoist and compressor plant in 1901.

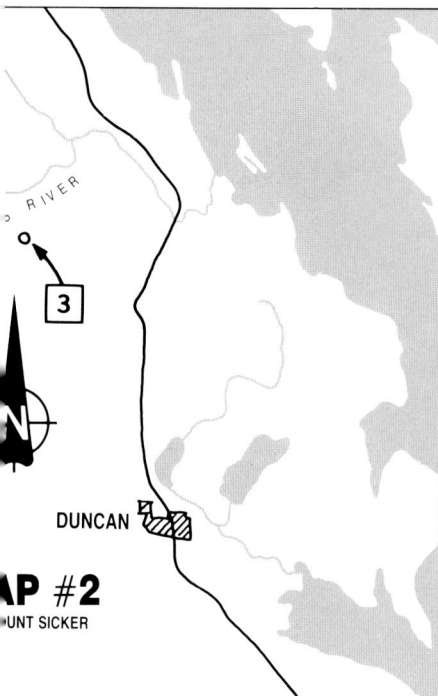

DUNCAN

3

RIVER

AP #2

UNT SICKER

tramway in the world.

Meanwhile, farther down the mountain, at Lenora, which had been employing up to 100 men and making regular shipments of ore, problems had arisen in the form of litigation which dragged on through the courts for more than a year. When the legal gun-smoke had cleared the company was in serious trouble. Its decrease in production, shrinking ore deposits and increased operating costs of its railroad meant the end. Within three years of entering production, the mining company was bankrupt. Its new homes and hotel, the fittings of which had been laboriously hauled in by horse-team and wagon, went on the block. The asking price for the cottages was $2 each; for the Mount Sicker Hotel, of the fine cuisine and scenic views, $8! The company's smelter at Crofton, idled for some time due to the lack of ore, was sold to a large mainland firm which used it to treat its own ores.

Fortunately for the Tyee, it continued to produce. During 1905, its peak year, the mine produced 3,047,835 pounds of copper, 102,677 ounces of silver and 5,956 ounces of gold and became the leading copper producer on the British Columbia coast. But there were clouds on its horizon, too. Although its shaft had reached a depth of 1,000 feet, the quality of ore had slipped alarmingly. Nevertheless, in 1906, it produced 23,832 tons of ore which yielded 2,115,617 pounds of copper, 77,085 ounces of silver and 3,776 ounces of gold. But in 1907 production fell dramatically as only 1,200 tons of ore were mined.

Even higher up the mountain, and somewhat to the east, the Richard III mine had entered production late in 1902, having arranged with the owners of the Tyee to ship its ore out by way of the latter's cable system to the Tyee-owned smelter at Ladysmith. By 1906 it was having troubles of its own. Despite extensive exploration it had been unable to locate a new ore body and its original seam gave every indication of pinching out. Faced with an uncertain future and shortage of capital, it was closed down while its owners decided what to do.

By 1907 the outlook for the Tyee was bleak. That same year the Vancouver Copper Company became interested in the old Lenora mine, shipping some 2,000 tons of ore before abandoning the venture. Then the dwindling stocks of paying ore, a high concentration of zinc (for which the smelters charged a penalty), and a drop in the price of copper closed the Tyee and Richard III.

Over the years, several attempts have been made to put the mines back into production.

Curiously, it is a matter of record that, had the original mine owners cooperated, rather than competed, they might have enjoyed longer runs. Instead they chose to duel and to duplicate, with lethal results for all. As early as 1902 a government mining engineer had mourned this lack of cooperation. Because the three major mines, Lenora, Tyee and Richard III, worked the same copper deposit they followed each other up the mountain-side, the Lenora at ground level, the Tyee somewhat above, and the Richard III considerably farther up the mountain-side. The owners of the upper mines could not take advantage of gravity in draining their workings, which were bedevilled from the beginning by water, as this would have required the agreement of the owners of the Lenora claim, and they were forced to the expense of installing an elaborate system of drainage pipes and costly electrical and steam plants to operate the powerful pumps required. For the Richard III and the Tyee this was one more nail in their coffins, and they

(Opposite page, top left) The stately Mount Sicker Hotel where miner Fred Beach open fire with his rifle after killing Joe Bebeau. With the closing of the mines the hotel and its ornate furnishings were sold for $8!
(Opposite page, top right) W.J. Watson, Superintendent of the Tyee Copper Co.'s smelter at Ladysmith, 1910.
(Opposite page, centre) Method of building roast piles, showing movable bridge and side-dumping cars in 1904.
(Below left) General view of Tyee Copper Co.'s smelter at Ladysmith in 1904.
(Below right) The remains of a building on Mount Sicker in the late 1970s.

Ore from the Lenora mine awaiting shipment on the Esquimalt & Nanaimo Railway in 1901.

gained little satisfaction from the failure of their arch-rival, the Lenora, as they were stuck with their pumps and pipes. Had they pooled their resources, as the Richard III and Tyee companies had agreed to use the latter's tramway and smelter, it is considered likely that all would have been able to continue indefinitely — certainly more economically. Instead, they agreed to disagree and died together.

This fact did not go unrecognized by later operations which, in their attempts to reactivate the old mines, worked them on a collective basis. However, it would appear that the original companies took the cream of the crop as, in more recent operations, the firms involved have become interested in the abandoned workings as newer and more efficient methods of separating the ores were devised. One serious attempt was made, half a century ago, to do what should have been done in the first place: connect the Lenora and Tyee shafts underground. But this attempt was soon abandoned. It has been estimated that $6 million in copper, silver and gold was recovered from the Mount Sicker properties over the years.

Like all rough-and-tumble frontier camps, those of Mount Sicker knew their share of tragedy. Unlike the search for coal, copper mining seems to have been reasonably safe as fatal accidents (here, at any rate) were few and far between. The most exciting of Mount Sicker's tragedies occurred at Lenora townsite in August, 1905, when Fred Beach, a jealous miner, shot Joe Bebeau, proprietor of the Mount Brenton Hotel. Although provincial police were soon at the scene and mounted an intensive manhunt, Beach eluded his pursuers, circled back to town, and fired several shots at the two-storey Mount Sicker Hotel. When a waiting posse emerged at the run, Beach, rather than be captured, turned his Winchester on himself.

Slowly, surely, the years took their toll of the old townsites. The magnificent little LMS had been stripped of its rolling stock and rails, and the old buildings fell victim to neglect and weekend lumber salvagers. Half a century ago, a newspaper columnist described a visit to the ghost camps of Lenora and Tyee: ". . .On the left an opening (in the trees) — an old barn, roofless; two or three skeletons of houses, the verandas broken, windows gone, steps fallen to one side; a broken door, a few carved posts still upright — the beginnings of the old town.

"Farther on, we round a bend. Here stands the deserted hotel, centre of the town. Now the great double doors hang lopsidedly against the door-frame, the windows are broken, glass, rags, bottles and lumber are scattered round. Inside is a large hall and the remains of room partitions.

"On the right is the barroom, with the counter standing crookedly against a wall. What stories it could tell of money, luck, misery and forgetfulness purchased over its polished top.

"In the hall is a wide stairway with banisters gone. Upstairs all the flooring has gone. Higher still is the framework of another story, a skylight still intact in the roof. Silence where once was noise. . . . Down the steps and on. We reach the dismantled shed of one of the mines. Some machinery and a rusty bucket still hang over the shaft, and outside are great banks of refuse. Farther on we find more houses, some in good state still. Paper yet hangs on the walls. Then another mine, and we turn back, for the road ends. . . ."

Still standing in 1932 were the old railway station, from which the ore was shipped; some of the shacks of the Chinese miners; the tumble-down athletic club; the house of the town doctor, where "a few drug bottles lie around, thimbleberry grows out of the floor and lichen crust the walls," the burnt remains and rusted bedsteads of Tyee's Brenton Hotel, and the old schoolhouse. Today, few of these survive, and most of the buildings yet to be found here are orphans of more recent mining ventures.

In 1935 a former resident of Mount Sicker recalled what it was like to live there.

"It was a humming place in those days," said Jack Potts, "with its three big mining operations all at once, the railway running up the side of the hill, conquering the grades by its ingenious switchback system, and the aerial tramline.

"I went up there to work as a diamond driller. I had one of the houses in the town. It was a nice place to live. The big hotel looking over the valley was a busy place. I worked on the Richard III, on the Tyee and also down at the bottom of the hill at Whisky Creek and Copper Canyon. Things were so busy in those days that the mines were running three shifts. . . It is interesting to us old-timers now to go up Mt. Sicker to see what is left now as the ghost town of what years ago was such a bustling and money-making place."

COPPER CANYON

Lenora and Tyee were not the only townsites on Mount Sicker, as the Mounts Sicker and Brenton Mines Limited had its own camp to the west. Here in the steep divide between mounts Sicker and Brenton, a motley collection of log and frame houses grew up about the company's mine and was know as Copper Canyon Camp. Besides the miners' houses there was a storehouse, shaft-house, framing shed and various other mine structures, but the camp never achieved the prominence, neither as a producer nor as a town, of its neighbours, Lenora and Tyee, which have come to be referred to us by the joint name of Mount Sicker.

Like its better-established sisters, the Copper Canyon operation laboured hard to make a go of it for several years. The Yankee, Victoria, Susan, Copper Canyon, Anoka, May, Star, Elmore and Victoria Fractional were some of the claims worked here at the dawn of the 20th century. Although the Mounts Sicker & Brenton Mines Ltd. were organized and originally financed in Victoria, like the others, it had had to go farther afield, in this case to Philadelphia, for funding — a fact of mining life which gave Mount Sicker an international flavour during its brief reign. ♣

Cassidy took great pride in its widely-acclaimed community. All buildings, streets and gardens were kept neatly trimmed. Single employees could rent accommodation in the famous 76-room California-style rooming house. Married employees could buy attractive company-built bungalows of three to 10 rooms.

VIRTUALLY nothing is left today of what once was proudly proclaimed to be the finest, most up-to-date mining settlement in Canada. Just crumbling concrete, acres of slag and wild fruit trees — silent monuments to the mortality of man and his creations — remain of the one-time coal town of Cassidy.

For the motorist with a few minutes to spare, the little ghost town just off the Island Highway, eight miles south of Nanaimo, offers an interesting half-hour's look around. Admittedly, Cassidy does not look like much now, and it is hard to imagine that these many acres of flat-land were once the site of a busy city — a city of solid, modern buildings, shady boulevards and well-tended lawns and gardens.

Also known as Granby, Cassidy was built in 1918 by the Granby Consolidated Mining, Smelting and Power Company. After test drilling on the Douglas coal seam in 1917 yielded satisfactory results, the Granby company started sinking the main slope on March 7, 1918. By the end of the year three parallel slopes had been opened and 16,958 tons of coal taken out in the course of development. According to an old newspaper account, Granby Colliery No. 1 was "the last word in coal mining during the brief years of its operation, and at peak production, around 1921 and 1922, 450 men were employed in connection with the works."

Rising above the Esquimalt & Nanaimo Railway (E&N) tracks to an elevation of about 150 feet is a sandstone ridge overlooking a bench bounded on the north by the Nanaimo River, and on the south by Haslam Creek. This location was chosen by F.M. Sylvester, the Granby company's vice president, as the site for the mine and residence district for employees. The principles of up-to-date industrial community planning were applied, setting apart 85 acres for a residential section, mine and plant sections, recreation grounds, streets, sewers, electric lighting, flower gardens, and sites for various buildings designated to meet the requirements of the company and its employees.

Taylor Engineering Company of Vancouver, contracted to design the site and construct the necessary buildings, allowed a plot of ground 50 feet wide by 100 feet deep for each residence. This permitted each occupant sufficient ground to grow fruit trees, vegetable and flower gardens.

Before the end of 1918 it was reported that 19 "residential houses for the employees have been built." In addition, there was "a general office, mine office, rescue station, mess-house, change house and lamp house; a two-storey rooming house containing 76 rooms; blacksmith shop, machine shop and carpenter shop."

The roadway plan had been arranged to accommodate 50 more residential houses in addition to a hospital and school. These bungalows, reported the *B.C. Mining Record,* "are of neat, varied designs, of the best construction, fitted with up-to-date sanitary and sewage systems, with water and electric light laid out on each. These houses have been constructed at a cost of from $1,500 to $3,000 each."

The residential houses were 150 feet apart, leaving 25 feet of lawn between the sidewalk and the front of the house. The

(Left) F.M. Sylvester, vice president and managing director of Granby Consolidated Mining, Smelting & Power Co., in 1918.
(Right) The main slope of the Granby Consolidated coal mines at Cassidy in 1918.

remaining 100-foot road allowance was taken up by the roadway, sidewalk and boulevard. The roadways were planted with a variety of trees, from which each street was named, such as Hemlock, Cedar, etc. The roadway and sidewalks were lighted by arc lamps.

The dormitory for the accommodation of single men was a two-storey, fireproof cement building, 100 feet by 140 feet, built in the shape of a double L. It contained 76 well-furnished rooms which were steam heated and had hot and cold running water. Each room opened either to the verandah of the ground floor or the balcony of the upper floor. The company supplied the furniture and bedding required and each employee had his own room. On the verandahs and balconies were window boxes of flowers which were carefully tended by men whose duty it also was to ensure that the lawns and boulevards were kept watered, and the flower gardens maintained.

The mess house, 75 feet by 125 feet, was a wonder of completeness and comfort. Entering the mess house was a long hall, with a row of wash basins on one side and hat and coat racks on the other. Each basin had hot and cold running water. The dining room was fitted with tables to seat six persons each. Waitresses served the bill of fair from the best supplies that could be obtained. Meals cost 40¢.

Off the mess house was the kitchen, with a long row of ovens. Electric dishwashers, slicing machines and other conveniences aided the work in the kitchen. A large brick oven was also provided.

The manager's residence overlooked the Nanaimo River, the bank of which was planted with all kinds of flowers and flowering shrubs. Between the residential district and the ridge to the east a recreational ground was laid out that provided tennis courts, running track, lacrosse, baseball, football and cricket grounds. A bowling green was also laid out.

Water was supplied to the town for domestic use and fire hydrants by twin Morris 4-stage centrifugal electric pumps which each had a capacity of 300 gallons. Operated by a 50-hp induction motor, these pumps raised water from a large pool in the Nanaimo River to two large storage tanks on the ridge to the east. Each tank had a capacity of 50,000 gallons and gave a pressure of 60 pounds to the square inch. Sewage was disposed of by way of septic tanks, for which the ground was well suited.

Between the sports ground and the mine were the concrete mine magazine, where the explosives were stored, the first-aid room, the lamp house, mine manager's office and the office of the overman and firemen. Other buildings included a carpenter shop, complete with rip saw, band saw, planner and boring and mortising machines; a machine shop, equipped with a large lathe, a pipe threading machine, two drill presses, emery wheel, planner and shaping machines; a blacksmith shop, fitted with two forges, swinging cranes and air compressor; a washery, installed in July, 1919; and a power plant consisting of two Badenhousen Stirling water tube boilers with a capacity of 290-hp each. The boilers and steam pipes were all packed with magnesite and asbestos to ensure the greatest economy of heat. The smoke from the boiler furnaces passed to a chimney eight feet in diameter and 150 feet in height.

Cassidy was always popular with the hardy coal-mining fraternity, its higher wages and comfortable, modern facilities drawing miners and their families to the new townsite. Despite "something of a dangerous reputation because of 'blow-outs' and gas 'bumps'. . .when jobs went a-begging elsewhere, there was always a waiting list at Granby."

The Granby company had spared no expense in constructing its model picture-book settlement of pretty bungalows, mine buildings and sawmill. By 1919 the plant had been completed. It had a capacity of 300,000 tons annually.

Cassidy was connected to the E&N mainline by a three-mile spur. Coal was shipped over the E&N to the docks of the Canadian Collieries at Ladysmith, where it was transhipped to its final destination. As business increased the E&N was confident that Cassidy would become one of the most important traffic centres on its route, and by 1919 had erected a new station there equipped for telegraphic and express business.

MAP #3

4. CASSIDY
5. MORDEN
6. EXTENSION
7. WELLINGTON

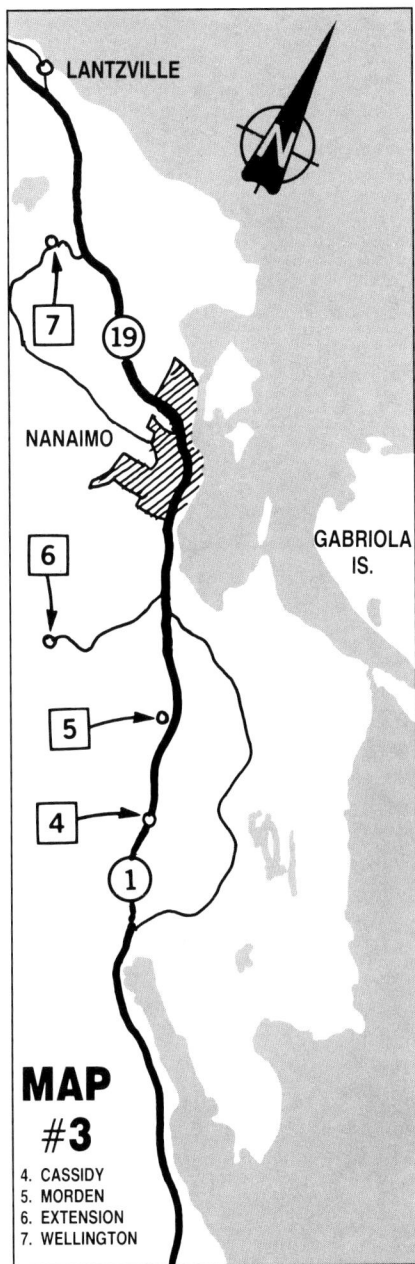

A view of Cassidy from the top of the bluff looking toward the manager's house.

As the years passed and Cassidy prospered and grew, new homes were built. The town had its own department store, theatre and paved streets. By 1928 the mine was producing 1,000 tons of the black fuel, coke for the hungry smelters at Anyox, in every eight-hour shift. The population had grown to more than 500 souls, 200 of whom toiled in the pits below.

The Granby Company looked after its employees; its original plans called for "hygienic arrangements to handle (500) men (to) be as perfect as modern methods will permit." Evidence of this was everywhere; the kitchen was touted as being "fly-proof"; all buildings were floored with "patent flooring" which was "easily washed and maintained in the cleanest (sic) of condition"; a disinfecting plant had been installed to "ensure the cleanliness of the furnishings of the dormitory"; and the change house, "equipped with every device such as hot and cold water, showers, baths, etc.," was conveniently situated.

The company and its employees took great pride in their widely-touted community, keeping all buildings, streets and gardens neatly trimmed. But, September 1932 brought the end. Some say the famous 10-foot-wide seam of coal gave out; others maintain it was the growing popularity of oil. Still others say that the mines became too dangerous. Actually it was a combination of all three factors, plus the depression, which spelled the death of Cassidy.

There was no turning back the clock. The powerful machinery which had been operating for 15 years wheezed to a final halt, leaving an eerie silence. The miners drifted away, abandoning their prized cottages to the care of a single watchman. A foreman in the mines until their closure, he was the only man kept on at Cassidy. Some years ago his son, then a lad, recalled how he had accompanied his father on his nightly rounds.

It was a spooky experience for a youngster, he said; with nothing more than flashlights to show their way amongst the vacant buildings which inspired a thousand terrors in his young mind, particularly when the wind was blowing and the buildings creaked and groaned.

The eeriest — and most thrilling — part of their rounds

(Above) The Cassidy Hotel, Cassidy, B.C.
(Below) The large rooming house at Cassidy.

came when they checked the shaft-house. In the feeble glow of their lanterns he could just see the length of rope which danced from a ceiling beam as the wind sighed through the structure. It was here that one of the Chinese mine workers, too old and ailing to find other employment, had taken his life upon the mine's closure. The rope was a chilling reminder, with its frayed end where his body had been roughly cut down. Some 40 years, and half a lifetime later, the foreman's son vividly recalled this unknown chapter in the Cassidy story.

In March, 1936, the "best company town in Canada" went on the auctioneer's block. Among the buildings disposed of was the two-storey, fireproof rooming house which had been specially designed to "give to the single men accommodation unexcelled by any building of its kind." The mess house also went on the block, as well as the model homes.

Built- to no fixed design so that the style of architecture would be the same "as may be seen in the newer portions of Vancouver and Victoria. . .they (were) handsome in appearance and contained every convenience, such as hot and cold water, bath, cooling chambers in connection with pantry, elec-

tric light, etc. These dwellings range(d) in size from 3 rooms to 8 and 10, the cost extending from $2,500 to $7,000 each."

The hammer fell mercilessly on the modern offices, the "fine stucco dining-halls," bathhouses and garages. Ironically, Granby Consolidated had built its structures so solidly that major buildings could not be removed intact, but had to be dismantled for their materials and fixtures. Only the five, six and seven-room bungalows could be transported, whole, to new locations.

Then the sewer and water pipes were unearthed, to be used elsewhere. The last of the mining machinery vanished in the smelter pots during the metal-starved war years.

After the wreckers had done their work the forest slowly reclaimed its own. By 1951 only gaunt concrete bones marked the site. The tall, arched walls of the apartment house resembled a Roman aqueduct. The 125-foot smokestack of the boiler house had gone, and the 125-foot-long mess hall had crumbled into complete ruin, except for the east wall, which stood forlornly amid the broken concrete and timbers.

The only residents left were a Mr. and Mrs. A. Ross. As caretaker for the property Mr. Ross lived in one of the abandoned offices. For almost 20 years the aging miner hand-worked a deserted shaft.

Today Cassidy is alone with its memories. Occasionally visitors poke about the few ruins in evidence, wonder what the ghost town was like, and leave. Few realize what stories Cassidy could tell.

We last visited Cassidy one bright July morning. A tired breeze wearily stirred the many apple trees, most still bearing fruit after all these years, that populate the gravelly plain. It did not take us long to snap our photos and head back to the car; there is little enough to keep one's interest, regrettably.

On the right side of the road is to be found the gaping foundation of a large building. Most of the floor has long fallen in although, in spots, it still is quite sturdy. A single wall remained upright in the church-like summer stillness.

This part of the former townsite has almost vanished. Besides the wreckers and ravages of time, the British Columbia Department of Highways has turned this bench-land into a massive gravel pit. Acres have been removed on both sides of the road. Huge slabs of concrete, once the foundations of large and attractive buildings, now piled haphazardly by provincial bulldozers, litter the landscape.

Large concrete ruins are to be seen at the timber-line also. Here, in the seemingly perpetual twilight, is the entrance to a mine shaft. Although the workings have collapsed far below and the dynamited remains of the adits have crumbled, deep in the maze and undergrowth one can yet see the rectangular outline of the old shaft.

Deeper in the trees other ruins can be found by following the old roads or railway grades. In a few more years the trees will have completely erased the former lanes.

Deep in the wood bordering the highway was a small log cabin built into the hillside. Actually it had been a cold storage house. Curio seekers have torn it apart and have dug up most of the surrounding earth. In their haste they overlooked long-fallen telephone poles with their old and prized insulators intact.

To the left of the road is a massive ore dump. Acres of the black waste are tumbled here; in some sections the highways crews have been busy rooting for road-fill. Only a few concrete towers, grotesquely naked, remain. These were loading chutes, built atop railway spurs. ♣

(Left) Morden Colliery during its peak.
(Right) This concrete ruin is all that remains of the boiler building and its twin smokestacks today.

A brief news item in January, 1972, announced that a skeleton of concrete in the South Wellington district, and 10 surrounding acres, had been set aside by the provincial government as Morden Colliery Provincial Historic Park.

Here, within two miles of the Island Highway, the aging pit-head works is perhaps the last surviving monument to an era when coal accounted for an important share of Vancouver Island's economy. But times have changed, the coal mines have long since vanished. Where once men laboured in the bowels of the earth, there is only water, the subterranean maze of passageways having flooded as soon as the pumps were shut down.

On the surface, bulldozers and dynamite have erased almost every trace of the adits and, but for a commemorative signboard in downtown Nanaimo, these mines which once employed thousands of men, and made the wheels of British Columbia commerce go round, have disappeared.

Probably the single exception is the pit-head remains of the Pacific Coast Coal Mining Company at South Wellington. As yet, the parks branch has not identified the site by sign or plaque, and the occasional visitor is left to guess as to its age and historical significance.

The former puzzle is answered by the ruins themselves as, further into the trees, a surprisingly handsome archway bears the brief legend, PCCM, and the date 1913. Fortunately the provincial Department of Mines and Petroleum Resources has a complete record of this ill-fated enterprise.

Most of Vancouver Island's productive coal has come from the famous Douglas seam which extends from Departure Bay southeast to Haslam Creek, just south of the Nanaimo River. Described in mining reports as being well-defined, and showing coal for almost its entire length, the outcropping has hosted several extensive operations, including such names from the past as Northfield, Protection, Southfield, Alexandria and Cassidy mines, as well as the cryptically-christened Nos. 1, 2 and so on.

No less than six miles long, the Douglas seam is composed of coal from beginning to end, but for fallow stretches, particularly between old Canadian Collieries' Nos. 5 and 10 shafts. According to mineralogists, "The Douglas seam floor is not regular but appears to be in valleys, ridges and knolls so that there are areas in this field where the coal varies from a few inches in thickness to 20 feet."

Due to this irregular surface, say the experts, even these barren pockets are likely to contain coal, although the "cost of exploring through these areas in prohibitive." In spots, such as old No. 1 Mine in downtown Nanaimo, the Protection Island pit, and at Morden Colliery, the seam is an amazing mile and a half wide, the richest area being about halfway down.

Work commenced on Nos. 3 and 4 shafts of the Morden mine in March 1912, the main shaft being nine feet by 16 feet and the air shaft being nine feet by 12 feet. Within months workers had reached the 550-foot level in the hoisting shaft, and the 450-foot level in the air shaft, and company officials hoped to produce coal by the end of the year.

However, it was not until April 19 of the following year that, 600 feet down, an eight-foot seam of coal was encountered. The work of connecting the shafts was almost completed when, on May 1, the United Mine Workers of American walked

Bunkers, loading plant and docks of the South Wellington mine at Boat Harbour in 1911.

off the job, forcing the company to let its new shafts flood.

During the yearlong shutdown surface workers completed the pit-head, a towering, grotesque frame of reinforced concrete straddled by a massive wheel by which the electric hoist was operated. From the surface, this concrete head-frame rose to a height of 74½ feet. Each of the main braces contained over 50 tons of concrete, and in the entire tipple and main frame there was approximately 500 cubic yards of concrete. The tipple had four tracks with two Marcus screens, one 64 feet long, the other 66. Both were five feet wide.

Despite its labour problems, Fiddick and Morden Collieries produced 77,000 tons of coal from its combined operations, the improvements to the Morden pit-head being described as "most modern (and) unique in this province." Built entirely of concrete and steel, it was fireproof and electrically-powered (both vast improvements over older operations), chute-feeding coal into waiting railway cars.

Utilizing the latest in technology, Morden Colliery boasted buckets of one-ton capacity, it being reported that "Doors are used in the shaft which automatically close after the loaded bucket passes through, so that nothing can fall down the shaft. After the bucket reaches the surface it is swung clear of the shaft by the bull chain and dumped down a chute into the railroad cars," steam being supplied by two 100-hp. boilers. "The plant is electric-lighted and cluster lights are suspended in the shaft just above the sinkers, which makes ideal conditions. The blasting is done by electricity, primers being used. The shots are fired from the power-house after all men are out of the shafts.

"This mine will be equipped with the most modern machinery, to handle an output of 1,500 tons a day of nine hours."

Annual mining reports of that era not only listed the total number of employees (86, including office workers and management personnel at No. 2 Mine, two miles to the east), and segregated them by skills (mechanics and skilled labour accounting for only 15 of the staff), but by race. The 1913 report noted that No. 2 employed 10 Chinese above ground.

Throughout 1915 and 1916, the work of getting the mine into production continued — fortunately without tragedy such as that which befell the company's No. 1 shaft, on February 9, 1915, when water from an abandoned shaft broke into the workings and drowned 19 men. Worked on a "pillar-and-stall" system, the young mine boasted coal "of a very good quality

for steam purposes," ranging from five to 20 feet in thickness.

By 1917, two new slopes had been driven at the 600-foot level, where 50 miners and four horses encountered coal ranging from four to 30 feet in thickness. To date top production was but 400 tons a day, although it was expected that the mine would soon achieve full operation. A government inspector reported the presence of some explosive gas, but that the timbering and roadways were in good shape.

At that time, however, it was admitted that the two main slopes were in "troubled ground, but it is to be hoped they will soon reach the coal again." A further problem had been encountered in November when a "a small heating took place in the old gob of (the original) slope, where the pillars had been extracted, which necessitated the putting-in of four concrete stoppings, thus sealing the section from the other parts of the mine."

No. 4 shaft was then used strictly for air supply and as an escape shaft, an elevator waiting to remove the miners at a moment's notice. That such safety measures were not to be considered luxuries is indicated by the fact that a government inspector noted the prevalence of coal dust throughout the workings and ordered it removed.

For 1917 Fiddick and Morden Collieries reported a total yield of 150,538 tons. By then its employees numbered 263, above and below ground. On the surface the company had made headway with its own standard gauge railway, which now stretched more than seven miles to Boat Harbour, where wharves, bunkers, and loading equipment were being completed in order to "accommodate the largest ocean-going steamers."

1919 saw Pacific Coast Coal Mines Limited boast capital to the tune of $3 million. But its Morden mine was yet in the growing stage: "Extensive development underground has been carried on during the year. The new shaft-bottom has been widened to allow the handling of more coal. The main slope has been driven through almost 900 feet of rock-fault and has again struck coal; although only four feet high, it is of very good quality. A main diagonal slope has been turned off the main slope, and will replace the old slope which has been abandoned on account of the haulage system. This new development is being pushed ahead as speedily as possible, as the main slope, striking this big fault, seriously delayed development."

The pit head and dumping chutes of the Morden Colliery as they appear today.

Although management had eliminated the coal dust hazard of the previous year, a provincial inspector ordered the suspension of all further work with explosives until improved ventilation removed the volatile gas he had detected in six locations.

Despite an increase in wages, the colliery's production was less than half that of the previous year.

For all of its problems and delays, the company remained confident of success and continued its expensive construction program. Latest developments at the site included the addition of 14 cottages which had been removed from South Wellington and rebuilt on the site. Also moved were two eight-room homes for the manager and "overman," and a complete boarding house with accommodation for 32. A large water tank from South Wellington improved the water supply system for the thirsty boilers.

Underground, the original slope, abandoned four years previously, had been reopened, cleared and retimbered and re-tracked for almost a quarter of a mile, and the ventilation system had been overhauled.

By year's end it was reported that the "new development of the mine has been pushed during the year as rapidly as labor conditions would permit (Morden apparently experiencing further difficulties with its employees), some 15,000 feet of solid work having been driven during the year. During the coming year it is expected a vigorous policy of development will be continued."

As for the mine's main entries, these were to be pushed vigorously as the company had no fewer than 1,800 acres of "virgin territory yet to be developed in this mine." According to the experts' calculations this area was expected to yield 1,000 tons of coal daily for 50 years.

But the Morden mine, for all of its owners' hopes and investment, was never to see full production. In 1921 the frustrated pit was closed — not seeing activity for nine years. In February of 1930 the Canadian Coal and Iron Company reopened the shaft and began pumping it dry. Once the powerful pumps had done their work miners encountered further delays due to local collapses and the formation of large caves on the main slope.

Nevertheless a small quantity of coal was mined in March, 3,000 tons being extracted by mid-August. Despite "some prospecting" on the west side of the shaft, the long-sought main coal seam was not located and the new venture, after having cleared and retimbered 700 feet on the main slope, was forced to shut down in the middle of August, 1930. When last the Morden mine is mentioned in annual mining reports, only a watchman was employed on the site, looking after the plant and equipment.

Today, little more than the concrete monster survives at Morden. In the trees an archway with the initials PCCB intrigues visitors. This concrete foundation is all that remains of the boiler plant which once contained three 150-hp Goldie & McCulloch high-pressure boilers. Individual settings connected these boilers to a 60-foot smokestack that was 66 inches in diameter. A smaller smokestack of nearly the same height stood alongside the larger one. Farther down the roadway, locals have turned the former railway grade and townsite into a garbage dump. It seems a sad fate for a mine which, ironically, yet has potential.

Due to the thoroughness with which the Douglas coalfield has been worked in past years, only two sites offer the possibility of coal in commercial quantities if the current increasing demand for coking coal justified the reopening of abandoned mines. "One of these," wrote an expert some years ago, "is in the area between the face of the old working of No. 4 shaft mine, in the Wellington-Extension field and the Nanaimo River...." After explaining the various factors involved, he continued: "The other possibility is the reopening of the Morden Mine. There are approximately 1,800 acres of coal lands in the Morden property. Only 70 acres have been worked.... From the 70 acres that has been developed approximately 7,000 tons of coal per acre has been extracted. If it could be proved that even 1,000 acres of the remaining 1,700 (sic) could produce 7,000 tons per acre, this would mean 7,000,000 tons of coal."

To prove this, present-day developers would have to embark upon an expensive diamond-drilling program. Making it all the more improbable that the Morden workings ever will come to life again, whatever the state of the world coal market, is the fact that test drilling in the vicinity of contemporary mines in the Douglas seam have indicated further work to be unfeasible; not because the coal is lacking in quality or in quantity, but because of the numerous barren pockets which cost time and money to clear. This, coupled with the enormous expense of pumping and repairing old No. 4, all on speculation, virtually guarantees that, here at Morden, coal is history. ♣

Morden 31

Extension

NOW primarily a residential and farming area, Extension can recall the day, three-quarters of a century ago, when its streets were crowded; when hundreds of homes and buildings stood here; when trains puffed regularly back and forth to Ladysmith, and all Island points north and south. Here, as at other Vancouver Island cities, the mining of coal spelled life and death to an entire township. When the mines closed, Extension slowly but surely ceased to be. As the miners moved away, many of the more substantial buildings were transported to nearby Ladysmith, port for Extension's bituminous coal. Today a towering slag pile and an occasional ruin among the grass and trees are the only legacy of a glorious past.

☆   ☆   ☆

As the turn of the century drew nearer, the Dunsmuir coalmining dynasty was becoming increasingly worried. Although its operations at Cumberland were progressing steadily, the famous Wellington pits, for long the mainstay — indeed, the star — of their empire were showing signs of being worked out. After so many years of exploitation, the extensive efforts necessary to tap the remaining coal were proving to be an expensive endeavour. In short, the Dunsmuirs were faced with having to make a new strike or shut down their mines, one by one.

It remained for a character named Ephraim "Edward" Hodgson to grant James and Alex Dunsmuir, in joint command of the mighty Wellington Colliery since their father's death, the reprieve they so desperately needed. He did this by discovering what appeared to be a large outcropping of coal, seven miles to the southwest of Nanaimo, on the southern slope of Mount Benson. Making his find all the more providential, at least in the eyes of the Dunsmuirs, was the fact that the deposit had been exposed to Hodgson's experienced eye by the falling of a tree. At any rate, the previously unknown seam, almost a foot wide at the surface, looked promising. As it also lay within the vast land grant of the Esquimalt and Nanaimo Railway (E&N) (another Dunsmuir creation), Hodgson approached James with news of his discovery.

The Dunsmuirs, of course, were excited. They became almost ecstatic when their engineers reported the deposit to be of excellent quality and of promising quantity. As it turned out, the "new" seam was an extension of the Wellington seam, which they had been working all along.

Throughout 1895 and 1896 the Dunsmuir engineers continued their surveys of the area, to find that there actually were two main outcroppings of top-grade coal which ranged up to 15 feet in width. Final analysis was that work should be pushed at all speed and the Dunsmuirs gave a green light to development.

One of the first projects to be completed was a standard gauge railway grade from the new mine site to the company's wharf facilities at Nanaimo's Departure Bay. Work was well under way when a competing coal company was granted a court injunction to have the Dunsmuirs cease in their plans to build their railroad right through their competitor's holdings. James Dunsmuir immediately took the issue to court, but without success; that august body ruled that he was not to encroach upon the New Vancouver Coal Mining and Land Company's property.

Although disappointed by this legal monkey wrench (particularly as the Wellington mines were fast approaching the point where they would have to be closed), Dunsmuir already had considered an alternative. When the court made its ruling he rerouted his railway to Oyster Harbour, an ideal bay 15 miles south of Nanaimo, and some 10 miles by rail to the southeast of his new mine.

As it happened, this setback proved to be something of a short-term blessing in disguise; by choosing Oyster Harbour as his shipping depot, Dunsmuir was able to route much of the proposed railroad along existing sections of the E&N right of way. This enabled construction to move ahead at a rapid pace. Meanwhile, at the mine site, work was so far advanced that his men already were preparing coal for shipment to the docks, which also were nearing completion at Oyster Harbour. There, large seaside bunkers were built to hold up to 8,000 tons of coal at a time. Chutes at each end of these bunkers would then disgorge the coal directly into waiting railcars for loading aboard ships and, for the first time on the island, into railcars carried aboard barges. This important advent in island mining meant that coal could be shipped directly by rail to mainland markets.

The result of all this development was the nucleus of a townsite to be known initially (due to the fact it was an extension of the Wellington coal seam) as Wellington Extension, then as Extension. At Oyster Harbour a second community began to grow around the new coal wharves: the future township of Ladysmith.

Less than four years after Hodgson's discovery on the slope of Mount Benson, Extension's mines were yielding 40,000 tons of coal annually. By 1899, production had increased tenfold, the resulting prosperity transforming both Extension and Ladysmith into thriving towns.

R.S. Wood, writing in the Ladysmith-Chemainus *Chronicle,* noted: "In addition to the 800 miners from the Ladysmith area working on a 3-shift basis at the Extension mines, between 30 and 40 men worked at the smelter, which treated ore from the Mount Sicker mines and shipped the concentrates to Tacoma for final processing. There were also a small shingle mill and an iron foundry in operation for brief periods that employed probably around another 30 people. . . ."

Curiously, Extension's expansion into a bustling township of its own was not according to plan. James Dunsmuir had hoped to discourage what modern-day developers would term "ribbon development." Ladysmith, decreed Dunsmuir, was to be the loading facility for Extension coal. At Oyster Bay, the building of homes for the miners was fine; at Extension this was a no-no. Nevertheless, more and more miners and others defied his ruling and began to establish about the Extension pit-heads. Before long Dunsmuir had to wave his hands in disgust and forget the matter as Extension blossomed forth

(Above left) The typical outfit of a Cumberland coal miner is displayed at the Cumberland Museum.
(Above right) Electric locomotive at mouth of mine tunnel, Extension, 1901.
(Below) This painting by artist Paul Grignon depicts a coal train at the Extension mine.

into a small town, despite the fact that many of the miners who worked in its pits continued to make their homes in Ladysmith and to commute daily by company train.

Coincidentally, as Ladysmith prospered the nearby community of Wellington withered. The old workings were phased out and sealed off and, by 1901, coal mining there was history. Most of Wellington's buildings were moved to its southern successor, Ladysmith. By this time Wellington's population had fallen from a high of 5,000, three years before, to 100.

Another major development in the Dunsmuir saga had occurred during this busy period with the death of brother Alex in 1899, and the assumption of the throne by James who, in the meantime, had added to an already heavy workload by being elected MPP for the riding of Comox. In 1900 he advanced to the highest provincial office, as Premier of British Columbia.

Then he began to slowly divest himself of his vast business interests. The E&N was sold in 1905, the extensive Union Colliery Company, which became known after further reorganization as Canadian Collieries (Dunsmuir) Limited, in 1910. It was under this title that coal mining came to the end of the road on Vancouver Island.

☆ ☆ ☆

At Extension the work underground had progressed steadily; particularly in Nos. 1, 2, 3 and 6 slopes, where a network of electric locomotives and trains of ore cars formed a miniature "trolley" system. As miners probed ever deeper into the mountain the electric railways for 1, 2 and 3 mines were connected so as to merge at a tipple almost a mile underground at No. 1. Altogether the little railroad extended more than two miles beneath the mountain. No. 6 was linked to the tipple by a mile-long narrow gauge surface line.

The years 1908 through 1912 were probably the period of greatest growth.

But the Extension mines did not escape misfortune. Disaster struck in 1901 when 16 men died. On October 5, 1909, 32 men were trapped underground in No. 2, the worst tragedy to occur here. Nine years before a head-on crash between a locomotive pulling empty ore cars and an E&N train on the mainline killed four members of the latter's crew. In 1912-13 the "big strike" spelled the beginning of the end for Extension and — almost — Ladysmith.

DAY OF TERROR AT COAL MINES: Strikers Attack Workers at Extension Where Shots Are Exchanged — Bystander is Wounded and May Die; Torch Applied to Colliery Buildings.

These were the shocking headlines which graced the *Colonist* on the morning of August 14, 1913, after miners, driven to desperation after months without a settlement, erupted in violence. Extension felt the brunt of their wrath and the militia had to be called in after rioters attacked mine property and the homes of strikebreakers.

After the soldiers restored order, much of Extension, particularly its Chinatown, lay in ruins. Reported the Victoria *Times:* "Houses of many mine employees that were not burned were wrecked and looted. In one house...a broken kitchen stove, a wrecked bed, broken chairs and tables, as well as the broken frame of an organ, are about all that remain of a miner's cottage. Glass covers the floor, remains of what were once clothes are strewn about, broken china and smashed tinware and granite ware, all sorts and ends of household utensils and clothing, lie in a chaotic mess on the floor, a picture of indescribable ruin. The picture will fit several houses visited by the mob and looters. From many houses almost everything of value has disappeared...."

34 Ghost Towns & Mining Camps of B.C.

Not until the strike was finally broken by strikebreakers did the mines of Extension resume operation. By 1919 they were again in full production.

But time was running out for Extension. With the start of the Depression in 1929 hundreds of men were thrown out of work. Two years later, on April 10, 1931, after having produced more than eight million tons of coal, the fabulous Extension Colliery was closed. As the exodus began, the tracks of James Dunsmuir's hard-won railway to Ladysmith were torn up, the docks and bunkers dismantled. For Ladysmith as well, the

(Above) Miners at the entrance to the mine, Extension, 1904. Note the number of boys, from about 10 years of age, and their "coffee-pot" lamps. Almost as fascinating are the mules. Many of these spent their working lives underground and lost their eyesight because of eternal darkness.
(Below) Westinghouse motor pulling ore train out of the mine at Extension.

closure of the pits meant disaster. By 1932 its population had sagged to 1,700.

But Ladysmith held on. In 1935 the Comox Logging Company became active in the hills behind the town and based its workshops and offices in Ladysmith. Ever so slowly more men found employment — not in the mines but in the woods. By 1938 the worst was over.

Alas, for Extension there was no reprieve, although as recently as 1950 some coal was being mined in the area, at the White Rapids Mine on the Nanaimo River. First explored by diamond drilling in 1943, it was here that Canadian Collieries made a last stab at coal mining for a further seven years. From the start it had been recognized that the White Rapids deposit was limited, only the construction of a logging railway in the area making it feasible in the first place. Then it too was shut down.

For the historically-minded visitor, Extension offers little more than marshy meadow-lands, abandoned railway grades and its towering ore dump. In the bush and fields are to be found some relics of a bygone era: the concrete ribs of a vanished building, a rusting ore cart almost buried in the grass, an old dump recently disturbed by a bottle collector. At the base of the coal dump a stand of cherry trees provides the early August visitor with a succulent treat in the form of small but delicious cherries as black as the pile of coal on whose slope they grow. Even in the dump itself tiny trees are shooting upward.

Although something of the community of Extension survives in the form of a store and dozens of homes and small farms, there is little beyond the coal dump to indicate to newcomers that, up until 50 years ago, this was a busy town, complete with substantial buildings and mines which provided employment for hundreds of men. It takes considerable scratching in the bush at Extension, and down on the flats, to find traces of its earlier prominence and small Chinatown.

Visitors find that a metal detector can be more of a curse than a blessing here; in half an hour its steady "beeps" indicate one piece of metal after another — all of them nuts, bolts and washers from the old railway trestles which were necessary to make Extension's swampy ground navigable. Deeper into the trees, there are signs of old dumps and some brick foundations; all of them disturbed in recent years.

In the village itself vacant lots between modern and original homes show where buildings have stood in the past. One house which is abandoned is enough to make a bottle collector drool: its well, not five feet from the roadway, has been used as a dump. Who knows what treasures lurk here! Always, it seems, they're in someone's front yard. . . .

There are no signs or plaques to tell of Extension's greatness. Only the files in the provincial archives and conversations with local residents can give some indication of a town built upon coal: a town where men died in mine explosion, and where martial law was declared and armed soldiers patrolled the streets during the worst of the labour strife which seems to have been part and parcel of the pioneer coal industry.

Although the town certainly has not regained anything of its former splendour, it has recaptured its respectability. As recently as December of 1948 a Victoria newspaper reporter described the orphan of coal as something of a wasteland: "Warped, unpainted shanties, many of them with their walls angling crazily and their windows cracked, make Extension, a few miles south of Nanaimo, the classical picture of a ghost town — except that people live in the tumbling huts.

"The town is dominated by a huge, black mountain of waste, the grim reminder that it was once the site of one of the richest bituminous mines in the country.

"The mine closed in 1931, but most of the 165 persons listed as living there still give their occupation as 'miner.' Some of them live in crumbling old hotels that must have throbbed with hearty frontier action in their heyday.

"Against the grey of the paintless buildings, fresh sawdust piled beside a mill off to one side of the town glares dazzlingly (sic).

"The residents are uncommunicative. At the approach of a car along the dirt-track roads, all but overgrown (with) weeds, children scuttle into their haunted houses.

"An old man found standing by a sagging fence was asked to tell what he knew about the town. He turned silently, his gaze swinging past the tottering steeple of a deserted church and stared, without answer, at the huge black waste pile, through lashless eyes."

Such, according to this source, was Extension in the late 40's. Today, as mentioned, it is a peaceful residential community nestled in a valley of green. A panoramic view can be achieved by climbing that "huge black waste pile." Numerous ruts indicate that it is a favourite of local motorcyclists, although, from the bottom, the climb looks to be almost sheer. However, once started, it proves to be no more than a steep incline and minutes later, puffing and clammy with sweat, visitors are at the top. Even on a summer Friday, Extension seems to be sleeping, it is so still, and one wonders how it was possible to build such a slag pile on the valley floor. Surely no railway ever climbed such a grade. Was the slag heaped here by an early-day conveyor belt method?

Proof of the steepness of the hill is provided by the descent when, unable to "brake," visitors are forced to gain speed until, by the time they reach the bottom, they are running full-tilt. Motorcyclists must be in their glory here!

The main tunnel to Nos. 1, 2 and 3 mines was here, and is revealed by some pilings of the mine railway. The mines themselves (Nos. 1, 2, 3 and 6 slopes) were in the valley; now the haunt of young horseback riders.

One cannot leave Extension without making brief mention of the Louis Stark case. This Negro pioneer settled in the Cranberry district around Nanaimo River near the end of the century. In due course, what with all the mining activity around nearby Wellington, Stark became aware of the fact that his homestead sat squarely upon a rich deposit of coal. Hefty offers were made for his land but Stark, who had left Saltspring Island under unhappy circumstances, was not interested.

Early in 1895 the body of Louis Stark was found at the base of a cliff. According to his nearest neighbour and friend — "Ed" Hodgson — Stark had spent the previous evening at Hodgson's cabin, playing crib. In fact, Hodgson said, he had walked part-way home with Stark after their game.

Police had other questions for Hodgson, the last man to have seen Stark alive. The biggest question was how Stark, who knew the trail by heart, could have fallen over a cliff when he would have had to climb over a jungle of deadfalls to do so. Although the police had their suspicions and arrested Hodgson for Stark's murder, the charge was dropped for lack of evidence.

This was one and the same Ephraim Hodgson who approached James Dunsmuir with news of a fabulous new coal deposit on the southern slope of Mount Benson. ♣

(Above) Time and again unrest shut down Vancouver Island coal mines and paralysed entire communities. During the big strike of 1912-13, Extension was the scene of a "reign of terror" when striking miners rioted. This photo shows the interior of a general store wrecked by the strikers.

(Left) No. 1 Company, 54th Regiment, leaving Extension in 1913. They had been called in to quell the riot by strikers.

(Bottom left & right) The coal slag at Extension is now a favourite for bikers.

(Above) Chinatown at Extension, showing some of the damage caused by the big strike, one of many which plagued the pioneer coal mining industry.
(Below) A general view of the community of Extension photographed from the top of the coal slag.

LIKE Extension, the three Wellingtons were virtually the creation of that mighty father and son team, the Dunsmuirs: Robert, James and Alex.

The story of Robert Dunsmuir, who rose from poor immigrant to business tycoon and "capped his career by building a story book castle for his bride," is undoubtedly more fascinating than fiction. Born in Hurlford, Ayrshire, Scotland in 1825, Dunsmuir had joined the Hudson's Bay Company (HBC) as foreman at its Fort Rupert coal mine. He arrived on isolated northern Vancouver Island in 1851 with his wife Joan, two daughters and infant son James, who had been born during their lengthy voyage from the Old Country. According to legend, the young miner had had to persuade his wife to venture halfway round the world by promising her that he would one day build her a castle. Whether this is fact or fairy tale he did just that.

After a rough voyage to Fort Rupert, Dunsmuir assumed his duties in the HBC's fledgling mine. Although this pioneer coal mining venture — British Columbia's first — failed, he remained with the fur company and eventually was transferred to oversee development of that firm's new Nanaimo workings. For some time he served as manager for the Harewood Coal Company, then went to work as a surveyor for the Vancouver Coal Company, successor to the HBC. While serving in this capacity, Dunsmuir became convinced that the coal he was searching for "lay in another direction and outside of the land owned by the coal company and he was determined to find it."

When not looking for outcroppings of coal, Dunsmuir took time to go fishing. It was while testing the reputation of Diver Lake, some five miles north of Nanaimo, that he began his meteoric rise to fame and fortune when he "came across a ridge of rock which I knew to be a strata overlying the lowest seam that as yet (had) not been discovered. I sent two men to prospect, who, two days later, discovered a three and a half foot seam of coal, 30 feet below top of the ridge, dipping south-east one foot in six inches."

Dunsmuir's chance finding of the Wellington seam was "the greatest discovery of coal since the one in 1849 (Fort Rupert)." Dunsmuir, having obtained government permission to pursue development beside Diver Lake, put his friend and fishing companion William Isbisiter, and James Hamilton to work sinking test holes. When they encountered the main seam, a slope was driven 285 feet into the coal, and the first 500 tons of black fuel removed by pick and shovel.

But, having gone this far — and convinced that the coal seam he had discovered was of superior quality — Dunsmuir faced the problem of convincing others. When HMS *Boxer* arrived in Nanaimo Harbour the canny Scot saw his chance, and convinced her master to conduct a test with 25 tons of his coal and 25 tons from the mines on Newcastle Island. After a fair trial, the ship's engineer reported the Wellington fuel to be superior for steaming purposes.

Thus armed, Dunsmuir approached several wealthy parties, among them Lieutenant Diggle of the *Boxer* who, for an investment of $10,000, became his partner in the firm of Dunsmuir,

Diggle and Company. By 1873, just two years after, their claims showed such promise that they were able to attract further wealthy backers to underwrite the costs of putting the mine into production; this, for half interest in what was to become No. 5 shaft. With this backing the company was able to replace its wagon road to the wharves at Departure Bay with a proper railway.

As the mine's output continued to grow, further improvements became necessary in the way of new hoisting gear at the pithead, and larger shipping facilities at tidewater. The injection of new capital permitted Dunsmuir to buy five miles of shoreline — more than adequate for expansion. By December 31, 1873, the Wellington mine of Dunsmuir and Diggle had yielded 16,108 tons of coal.

Not all proceeded perfectly to plan, however, as the unstable international coal market forced the company to announce a wage cut of 40¢ per ton. Although work on the new No. 4 shaft proceeded, the miners downed tools until a compromise was reached. By December of 1876, despite a fire in No. 5's upper level which had forced a shutdown, the tonnage of coal produced had soared to 60,000.

Two months later the miners struck again, this time complaining about dangerous working conditions. According to a report in the provincial archives, the miners also demanded a pay increase of 20¢ per ton: "The management refused and a bloody strike broke out, strikebreakers (were) imported, (and) the militia brought in to enforce martial law. Strikers (were) evicted from the company homes, battles between strikers and strikebreakers were numerous, arrests (made) by the score, (which resulted in the) convictions of some, (while) others (were) freed." The coal company inserted an advertisement in the Nanaimo *Free Press* to the effect that none of its striking employees would ever again grace its payroll. Six months after, the strike was settled and the miners gained a raise in their pay.

Dunsmuir, finally confident of success now that the company enjoyed a ready market in San Francisco, built the first and humblest of the family mansions, Ardoon at Wellington. Dunsmuir also felt confident enough to buy out two of his partners and, in 1879, Dunsmuir, Diggle and Company absorbed its nearest competitor, the South Wellington Colliery Company which had been active, in a sense, in their backyard. Although the South Wellington Colliery had two mines in operation as well as its own narrow gauge railway, it had been troubled by labour and financial woes for some time. Its addition to the Dunsmuir and Diggle stable greatly strengthened the partners' position and they proceeded to invest in major improvements to the combined enterprise.

On December 6, 1878, tragedy struck the Wellington Colliery when a Chinamen named Kong Sing was killed on an incline on the tramway. According to the evidence taken at the Coroner's inquest, Sing, a brakeman, was in charge of the "run," and at the time of his death he was riding on the front car going up the incline. When near the top, the cars were derailed by an iron rail which had been laid across the track.

The towns of North Wellington (above) and South Wellington (below) were located near Departure Bay, opposite to the Nanaimo Harbour, and less than a mile distant from each other. In 1884 North Wellington had a population of 1,200. Besides the residences of the miners, there was a public school and Methodist church. South Wellington consisted of the company's works and the cottages of the miners and other employees. It is also where the extensive wharves and coal bunkers of the company were located.

Sing was thrown off and three or four cars passed over him. He was so badly mangled that he died almost instantly. The inquest proved "beyond doubt" that the rail could not have been placed there accidently, but had been ". . .placed there purposely, by some person or persons unknown." Who had placed the rail there and why was never discovered.

Edward Prior, Government Inspector of Mines, expressed his concern that the habit of women and children riding on the cars running on this 1,000-foot incline would, sooner or later, lead to a very serious accident. Colliery officials constantly warned against this practice, and in fact, printed warnings were conspicuously posted, but some persisted in gambling with their lives.

Although predictions had been made that 1879 would be a record year, production sagged below expectations due to an underground explosion. The disaster, which occurred in Wellington Colliery's No. 1 mine on April 17, claimed the lives of seven white men; John Dixon, William Rennie, John Hoskins, Reuben Gough, Edward Campbell, Apollis Damey and Louis Prelee. Four Chinese were also killed, but in the typical attitude of the day that Chinese were worthless, their names were not included in the government reports.

The first indication of impending disaster occurred on April 15 when the coal in Horne's heading on No. 10 Level caught fire. Strenuous efforts were made during that night and the following day to put it out. Because thick smoke prevented men getting near the fire, it was decided to change the direction of the flow of air. To prevent the air from going any further than the heading, a curtain was placed across the level around 6 o'clock on Wednesday morning. Dixon, the overman, and one of the men subsequently killed, had gone into the level some five or six times between the time the curtain was put up and 2 p.m. the same day to determine if any gas was accumulating there. Each time he reported all clear. By 3 p.m., the men seemed to have the fire under control, there being no flames visible. However, as a precaution, water continued to be poured on the coal in the event the fire was smouldering underneath.

On Thursday morning, between 2 and 3 o'clock, Churchill, the fireman, while making his round of inspection, went into Horne's heading and the two next stalls inside, but did not go any further into the level because of the caution on the curtain. In chalk, was the warning: "No one allowed to pass here — Fire!" Dixon had been left in charge of the mine and

(Left) No. 5 shaft, Wellington, in 1890.
(Opposite page, left) James Dunsmuir (top) and Alexander Dunsmuir (bottom), sons of Robert Dunsmuir.
(Opposite page, top right) Craigdarroch Castle. Robert Dunsmuir had promised his young wife that if she accompanied him to Vancouver Island, he would one day build her a grand castle. By 1887 he had become one of the richest men in Canada through his coal mining ventures, and began plans for the building of the castle. No expense was spared in the 35-room, four-storey, fortress-like structure. It was constructed on a hill surrounded by 27 acres of terraced gardens, orchards and oak groves. The ceilings of the main floor were painted with birds and bees; fish and game in the dining room. Unfortunately, Robert Dunsmuir died on April 12, 1889 without ever having lived in his dream castle.
(Opposite page, bottom) Nanaimo 1910. This Paul Grignon painting depicts the port city during the era when coal was its major industry.
(Below) This Paul Grignon painting depicts a colliery engine and coal cars at Wellington during its prime.

he had been cautioned several times by the manager not to allow anyone to pass through the curtain.

When the explosion took place about 7 o'clock, Dixon and three Chinamen were found killed a long way inside the curtain. The rest of the white men who were killed were all outside the curtain. One Chinamen was missing. On April 19, after recovering all the bodies except the missing Chinaman, this part of the mine was flooded.

After a lengthy inquest, Government Inspector Prior issued his report, which concluded that the missing Chinaman had been responsible for the explosion. He wrote:

"On perusing the evidence of William Roberts, you will notice that he states he told two Chinamen to go to work in No. 83. This place was in No. 7 level. When the pit was in proper working order one of these Chinamen was in the habit of working in No. 82, this being the face of No. 10 level, and the point at which the explosion took place. This man had worked the previous day in No. 83, having been taken there by Roberts. After the explosion, all the bodies were recovered with the exception of this man, who could not be found anywhere. As I have before mentioned, the mine was flooded, and it was not until the 9th January, 1880, that the water was pumped out sufficiently to allow men to get into No. 10 level. On going in they found the body of the missing Chinaman laid within some fifty feet of the face of the level, and terribly burnt. I went down and saw him before he was moved. To my mind this, in connection with the state of the level, is conclusive proof that he was the man who fired the gas. The only reason I can give for his going there is that he understood Roberts to tell him to go to No. 82, and not, as really was the case, to No. 83. No 82 being his usual working place, and the two numbers being somewhat similar in sound to the ears of a Chinaman, it may easily be seen how the unfortunate mistake happened."

As for the reason Dixon and the other Chinamen were inside the curtain, Prior concluded that when Dixon reached No. 10 level, he was met by two Chinamen who were supposed to have gone to Level 7. They told Dixon their ". . .partner had gone inside the curtain. Thereupon Dixon, suspecting the danger, rushed in with his two Chinamen in order to overtake him and bring him back, but before they could get within shouting distance, the flame of his lamp had ignited the gas which must have been lying there."

Less than a year after this tragedy, disaster struck Wellington with a vengeance when 75 men were killed in a second disaster. This time, production was brought to a standstill until the mine could be cleared of bodies and debris, and repairs could be made. Among alterations made after the disaster was an improved ventilation system.

In less than nine years, despite tragedy and strike, under Dunsmuir's strong hand the Wellington pits yielded 200,000 tons, most of which was shipped to San Francisco. When Dunsmuir bought out his first and last partner, Lieutenant Diggle, the historic company was renamed Robert Dunsmuir and Sons Limited. By this time James and Alex were his right and left hands and quite capable of helping to oversee operation of the company's five mines at the two Wellingtons.

In the meantime, a comparative newcomer to the Island coal mining scene, the East Wellington Colliery, had opened on the Dunsmuir's southeastern flank with two new shafts. Like the South Wellington Colliery, the East Wellington Colliery experienced hard going, its claims being cursed with outcroppings of rock. This, however, did not dissuade them from building their own narrow gauge railroad from the pitheads to Departure Bay. Then the company abandoned one of its pits so as to concentrate on the second. This time their efforts were rewarded when the coal seam, although extremely narrow, proved to be of exceptionally high grade — promising enough to encourage the firm to sink a third shaft. By 1886 the East Wellington Colliery was at last in production and

(Left) Capt. Wadham N. Diggle, who, for an investment of $10,000, became Robert Dunsmuir's partner in the firm of Dunsmuir, Diggle and Company.
(Right) The Pacific Coast Coal Mining Co.'s works at South Wellington c1910.

(Above) Wellington's Abbotsford Hotel. It later achieved fame of sorts when it was transplanted to Ladysmith as a boarding house and office for the Comox Logging and Railway Company. Demolished in the 1970s, it was one of the last survivors of "old" Wellington.

(Below) A street scene at Wellington in the 1890s.

making a nominal profit for its herculean efforts.

Not all had been going perfectly for Dunsmuir and Sons either as, on January 1, 1885 an explosion in No. 4 started a fire which killed four men and played havoc with both Nos. 3 and 4 (then joined) for years until a firewall was installed between the mines. On January 24, 1888, the busy No. 5 shaft at Wellington was rocked by an horrendous underground explosion. Of the 168 men working below at the time of the blast, 91 made it to safety. The following year disaster struck the Dunmuirs personally when patriarch Robert died at the age of 64.

Included in his great legacy was the worst strike in the company's history, James having refused to negotiate further with miners who demanded a 10 per cent increase and an eight-hour workday. This time the difficulties lasted all of 18 months and again required the services of militiamen to quell disturbances between strikers and strikebreakers. On November 13, 1891, the strike was at last ended when the miners agreed to return to work.

There were further difficulties over the years: despite all, the Wellington Colliery continued to prosper. With its purchase of the financially-plagued East Wellington Colliery in 1895 it became virtual master of the Vancouver Island coal industry, its only major competitor at this time being the New Vancouver Coal Mining and Land Company at Nanaimo, successor to the Vancouver Coal Mining & Land Company.

It was at this point that James, in personal control of the Island operations since Alex assumed charge of the San Francisco office, and painfully aware that time was running out for the Wellington mines, became interested in reports of a new coal strike on the southern slope of Mount Benson. Then

plans were made for the birth of what was to become known as Extension.

On March 17, 1899, the miners were informed that the Wellington Colliery would be shut down within two years. In October, 1900, the last ton of coal was removed from No. 5 shaft and full-scale coal mining at Wellington was finished — just 30 years since Dunsmuir's discovery near Diver Lake, and just seven years since the younger "Wellington Townsite" was incorporated. For a time the community of Wellington had boasted a population of 5,000 souls and was larger than Nanaimo. But with the passing of coal those fine buildings and homes which had survived the fire of March 17, 1899, were torn down or moved to Ladysmith. Those remaining were sold as they stood — for $30 each.

Today "only the refuse heaps, rail track beds, empty lots, foundations of buildings, show where a house, hotel or a locomotive once stood." Gone also are the opera house, destroyed by fire, and the town's cinder track, which had been famous throughout the Pacific Northwest for its bicycle racing.

With the belated shutting down of No. 10 at South Wellington in 1951, the coal mining saga of the three Wellingtons was officially closed. Although small-scale and sporadic efforts were made over the years at various locations of the old workings, these amounted to no more than a picking of the bones. For the Wellingtons, Extension and Nanaimo, King Coal was dead. ♣

(Top) This new home in Nanaimo was discovered to be over a deep old shaft. The house directly opposite had its lawn cave in from the same cause. Numerous old shafts, their precise location unknown, are scattered throughout the area.
(Left & below) Two interior views of Craigdarroch Castle. The massive oak stairway was built in Chicago.

Red Gap

(Above) A view of the Straits sawmill, Nanoose Bay. (Below left) The Arlington Hotel, Nanoose Bay.

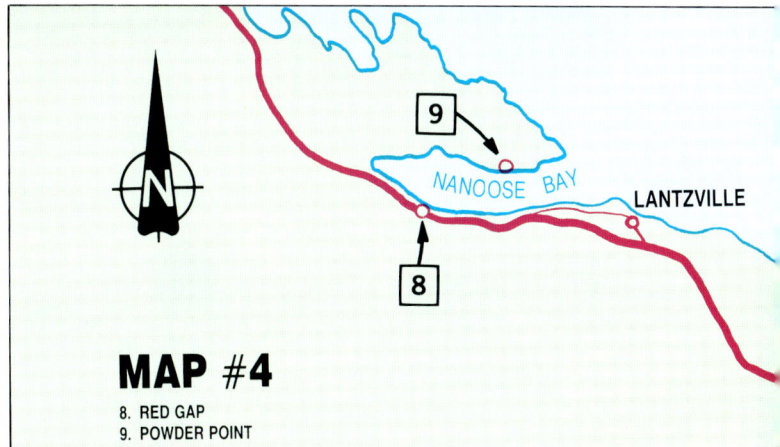

MAP #4

8. RED GAP
9. POWDER POINT

TWENTY miles north of Nanaimo, and five miles south of Parksville, Nanoose Bay offers not one but two ghost town sites, one on each side of this large, sheltered harbour.

A stubble of worn pilings beside the Island Highway marks the brief existence of the lumbering community of Red Gap. Situated in a draw on the opposite (west) side of the road, Red Gap served as the residential satellite of the Straits Lumber Company.

Originally logs were shipped by railroad to Nanoose from as far distant as Coombs, by the Walter Forbes Logging Company. But, in 1912, the bay became the site of a modern sawmill, the brainchild of Joe and Max McKercher. They were succeeded by new owners, the mill becoming a joint project of the Newcastle Lumber Company and Merchant Trust. They, in turn, were superseded by Frank Pendleton Sr. and family, in 1917, the second team of owners having suffered bankruptcy.

It was as the Straits Lumber Company, and under the steady management of the Pendletons, that the sawmill on the western shore of Nanoose Bay, immediately beside the Esquimalt & Nanaimo Railway (E&N) line, became a leading producer of fine Vancouver Island lumber.

Soon ships from around the world called at Nanoose Bay to load lumber from a small fleet of scows (the harbour not being deep enough to allow ships to dock alongside the mill) which serviced them. Japan was the primary customer. An old Empire Stevedoring Company accounting of ships loaded here in the years 1915, 1922 and 1923 reveals that the pioneer longshoring firm loaded 29 ships, among them the *Yoshida Maru* and the *Erie Maru.*

(Above) Richard P. Wallace and his wife at their farm at Nanoose Bay c1913. Wallace served as Justice of the Peace.

The strong international demand for Nanoose-cut lumber created more and more jobs; to accommodate its growing staff, Straits Lumber built a small settlement at the mouth of a creek, adjacent to the mill.

Because the E&N and the Island Highway, such as it was, ran between the beach and the base of a steep embankment, the architects had no choice but to build the camp on a network of pilings that straddled the mouth of a creek. Every home and outbuilding — even the sidewalks — were constructed on this artificial foundation across the gulch.

The settlement's distinctively American-sounding name was inspired by the then popular fictional book, *The Ruggles of Red Gap.*

Besides the company store, post office, school and boarding houses, the main community consisted of private homes. Similar, smaller conclaves were built beside the railway tracks for the Chinese, Japanese and East Indian employees.

By the mid-1930s, despite the Great Depression, the sawmill at Red Gap was booming, old photographs showing acres and acres of log booms in the bay, beneath a pall of smoke from the mill's sawdust burner and smokestacks. "The mill is working overtime these days," popular newspaper columnist Arthur Mayse wrote of the settlement in 1935. "As we pass, the shriek of saws and the hiss of escaping steam is deafening. Great, dripping logs crawl endlessly, up the chute to disappear in the busy dimness behind."

"On the other side, between the rails and the highway, are the houses of the Chinese workers, each with its small, gay garden of flowers and vegetables. At the Hindoo boarding house a picturesque well-sweep dips its wooden bucket creakingly beside a chickencoop painted white and pink and blue

to scare away devils. . . ."

Continued demand for Nanoose-milled lumber (Straits Lumber became well-known for its "Jap squares") saw more and more ships call during the quarter of a century that the Pendletons were in command. Almost from the beginning, Japan had been the largest importer of lumber milled here, and this finally proved to be Straits Lumber's downfall. With the infamous attack on Pearl Harbour in December, 1941, and Japan's entry in the war, the Nanoose firm lost its best customer.

Within months, Straits Lumber was out of business. Milling ceased in 1942 and, the following year, the order was given for its dismantling. Demolition was completed well ahead of schedule when a spark from a cutting torch ignited a fire which razed much of the operation. (A previous fire had significantly damaged the mill two years before.) The Pendletons moved to the mainland, and the old millsite was used by a succession of smaller, "gyppo" operators until the early 1950s, when all sawmilling here formally ended.

At the peak of its career, for a period of three years, the Straits Lumber Company had earned the distinction of having the biggest mill in the entire Pacific Northwest.

Red Gap, of course, did not long survive its reason for being and, today, there is virtually no trace of the cabins which had straddled the mouth of the draw, opposite the mill. Over the years, the Island Highway has been widened several times, the most recent surgery having cut well into the embankment. Consequently, Red Gap is gone and, but for a few historically conscious residents of the Nanoose Bay area, forgotten.

This oversight is to be corrected by the placement of a marker. ♣

Powder Point

ACROSS Nanoose Bay from Red Gap was the site of another boom-and-bust phenomenon. However, whereas Red Gap owed its existence to sawmilling, the industrial development and resulting townsite at Powder Point was created by the need for high explosives.

Today, but for a spattering of modern homes, and what has become a Canadian Armed Forces preserve, this peninsula remains little changed from the way it must have appeared to pioneer John Enos, who settled at Notch Hill in 1862.

Despite its pastoral serenity, Powder Point had not always been peaceful. About 1823, it is believed, an Indian massacre occurred here, excavations some 90 years after having uncovered as many as 40 skulls and human bones; all of the former had been crushed by a blunt object, such as a tomahawk.

Other settlers, such as U.E. Dickenson and Dick Wallace, soon followed John Enos. Ultimately, the area attracted industrial development in the form of a brickyard, between Powder Point and Schooner Cove.

But it was in 1912 that true progress arrived in the form of the Giant Powder Company. Even in those days, this was a very ambitious undertaking, the project sprawling over hundreds of acres. The reason for this widespread arrangement of buildings was the omnipresent fear of explosion. Consequently, the black and white powder works were built well apart so as to minimize the threat to life and damage to buildings should there be an accidental blast.

At the point, a machine shop, railway shed (to house the narrow gauge "locie" which connected the various works and buildings) and wharves were constructed. It was during excavations for the powder house and oil tanks that remains of the victims of the long-ago massacre were unearthed.

The nearby townsite consisted of 15 houses, among them the assistant superintendent's residence, apparently the size of a mansion, and cottages for the workers. A 25-resident Chinese ghetto was situated further inland, ostracized in the usual manner of the times.

When I visited the site in March, 1983, the freshly bulldozed ruins of the black powder manager's home were still smouldering. Situated on a rise just outside what is now Department of National Defence property, the house overlooked two of the more imposing ruins that survive of the historic enterprise.

These are the three-sided concrete foundations of the two mills where the black powder (charcoal) was ground and mixed with sulphur. The fourth wall of each mill, long gone, would have been of frame construction so as to funnel the force of any explosion in the desired direction. In the late 1940s a small sawmill operated here; it, too, has been razed and only some farm buildings of corrugated iron remain. But these were also fated for demolition as the property was being subdivided.

On the other side of the roadway, beyond the manager's house, was the three-storey, gabled boarding house. With its large verandah, second storey balcony and observation tower, it was unquestionably an imposing structure, as revealed by an old photograph. Now only a concrete slab marks it location in an overgrown pasture. Three large water tanks, spring-fed,

have also disappeared. The Chinese settlement was situated further into the trees, between the boarding house and the townsite.

Cattle trails, old logging roads, pipelines and the original narrow gauge railway grades crisscross the area, linking the old and new. The term "narrow gauge" was a literal one, as the former right of way seems little wider than a footpath.

Most striking of the surviving structures is the long, low-gabled white powder storage shed. Unlike the ruins previously described, this yet solid building remains in service, within the naval testing grounds. Joint Canadian-American underwater weaponry tests are conducted here and permission to enter the grounds must be obtained, in writing and in advance, from the Commanding Officer, CFB Nanoose.

Cast in solid concrete, the old building bears a date of 1913. Just how well it was made is dramatically illustrated by the fact that it survived the infamous blast of the "dope house" (white powder works, where nitroglycerin was made), which occurred but a few yards away, on New Year's Day, 1918.

Because of the holiday, only foreman J.O. (Jack) Cross and an unidentified Chinese workman were on duty when 50 tons of the liquid explosive were detonated. The magnitude of the blast can be gauged by the fact that the concussion was heard and felt as far off as Ladner, on the lower mainland, and residents of New Westminster thought that there had been an earthquake. Of Jack Cross and his workmate, only a blackened hand was found.

The explosion site is easily distinguished from among other ruins by a number of steel girders, still embedded in their concrete footings, that litter the scene; all have been twisted and torn by an incredible force. No bulldozer could have mangled steel to this extent.

As mentioned, the adjacent powder house survived; quite likely because it is situated at the foot of a small bluff, at roof level to what had been the dope house, which seems to have blown to seaward, undoubtedly thanks to its three-sided design of concrete and wood.

The white powder plant was rebuilt but, in little more than a decade, the Giant Powder Company's half-million dollar investment, then a staggering sum of money, was all but written off with the firm's absorption by what was to become Canadian Industries Limited (C.I.L.). This merger saw the explosive plant moved to James Island, near Sidney.

Among the casualties was the little townsite with its panoramic view of Nanoose Bay. Here, married employees had enjoyed most modern conveniences, including free firewood, for $8 per month. The company even installed its own power, fresh water and ice-making facilities. Single employees were accommodated in the massive boarding house, the Chinese in their shacktown. Management never did provide a school as employees' children were bussed to public Brynmarl School in an open jitney.

All production of gunpowder, dynamite and nitroglycerin ceased here in 1925. Upon the transfer of most employees to James Island, the extensive works at Powder Point were sealed. Most, as noted, have fallen victims of neglect, salvagers and, more recently, demolition efforts of a development firm which plans a large scale subdivision here. The navy also destroyed many of the old works on its property.

A prominent survivor of the Giant Powder Company is the large, handsome house near the junction of Northwest Bay and Powder Point roads. Well preserved, and enlarged, this residence originally served as the gatekeeper's cottage. ♣

The massive coal wharves at Union Bay. Note the ships waiting to load Cumberland coal.

ONE hundred and forty miles north of Victoria the Island Highway offers a clear view of the historic Canadian Collieries Limited property at Union Bay. Sadly, its clutter of buildings and the mammoth dock, one of Vancouver Island's oldest and most prominent landmarks, is no more, having been demolished in 1966. Nothing remains of the internationally known coal shipping terminal but smashed concrete and a small, rolling desert of coal chips and gravel.

Gone are the massive railway trestles, loading chutes and docks; the buildings and repair shops; the famous coke ovens which glowed red around the clock. Long known to thousands of passing motorists, the demise of this port formally closed one of the most important chapters in Vancouver Island, and provincial, history. . . .

Ever since 1869, when Sam Cliffe had learned about black outcroppings from an Indian, the Comox district was suspected of being rich in coal. Cliffe and his associates staked claims on Coal Creek, but when they ran out of funds they were forced to sell out to coal baron Robert Dunsmuir. Dunsmuir incorporated the Union Colliery Company and began operations in the spring of 1887. They found coal and started two slopes, which they drifted in for about 500 feet. For nearly all of that distance, the coal, averaging fully three feet in thickness, was of good quality and very hard. Although no coal was shipped in 1887, it was expected there would be a large output by the end of 1888.

While work at the mine was progressing, engineers were busy surveying and locating a line for a railway and other works required for the transport of the coal to a port, from which it would be transhipped to markets around the world. Cliffe and his partners had originally selected the future site of Royston as the shipping terminal, but Dunsmuir realized that its harbour was too shallow for his needs and he instructed his engineers to divert the proposed railway to the deep water bay to the south. Once the survey was completed, hundreds of men were employed in the construction of a standard gauge line, including one very large Howe truss bridge over the Trent River.

The harbour where the 11-mile line ended was named Union Bay, and at that location the largest wharves in the province were constructed. According to the *Minister of Mines,* "Four of the longest ships could tie up at the principal shipping wharf, and all be loading coal at any stage of the tide. At the other large wharf freight can be discharged and loaded directly on the cars; at the same time coal may be loaded into vessels if required."

In 1888, the Union Colliery employed 90 whites, earning $2.50 to $4 per day, and 150 Chinese, who earned $1 to $1.25. This year also saw the recording of the mine's first fatality when Nat Kilpatrick was killed in an accident with coal cars on No. 1 slope. The value of the Company's plant was listed as $25,000, and included a steam sawmill of considerable capacity which was erected near the mine.

By 1889, the No. 1 slope had been extended to about 2,000 feet, despite considerable trouble with faults of one kind or another. Four levels ran from this slope, one to the south side and three to the north. Although some gas had been detected by the mining inspector, he was confident that there was little chance for it to accumulate. The mine was well ventilated with 22,000 cubic feet of air circulating per minute. The mine was also free of dust.

Work on No. 2 slope, about a half-mile south of No. 1 slope, was about 40 feet deep. However, although a lot of prospecting had been done at this location, the coal had not yet been pinpointed. Despite this, the mine produced 31,204 tons in 1889, and now employed 132 whites and 182 Chinese. The only death this year occurred on October 30 when Ah Yeut fell from a trestle near No. 1 slope. He died the next day.

In 1892, despite some of the Company's slopes being inactive due to a decreased demand for coal, 66,556 tons were produced. The Union Colliery now employed 250 whites, 70 Japanese and 200 Chinese. The whites had received a pay raise and were now paid $3 to $4.50 per day, but the Japanese and Chinese were still only getting $1 to $1.25. The company's assets, meanwhile, which included 12 miles of standard gauge railway, 4 locomotives, 100 25-ton coal cars, a diamond drill, three stationery engines, three steam pumps, a steam sawmill, two wharves and a pile driver, was now valued at $100,000.

At Union Bay, meanwhile, in addition to the shipping wharves, there was also a well-equipped Luhrig coal washer, a coking plant consisting of two batteries, each of 100 beehive ovens, and large and suitable coal bunkers. A brickyard was also established to manufacture firebrick from the Cretaceous fireclay taken from the coal mines at Union Colliery. This brickyard produced the brick and blocks used in construction of the coke ovens erected there and later produced firebrick for the general market.

The coal was elevated into the Luhrig washer, which had a capacity of 500 tons for 10 hours. After being washed, the coal was stored in a large coal bunker that had a capacity of 4,000 tons. From there the coal was placed into cars and conveyed by different branch lines over the coke ovens, where they emptied their contents as desired. Each of the beehive ovens contained about five tons to a charge, which produced about three tons of coke. There was also a battery of three egg-end boilers, which furnished motive power for washer and brickyard.

The actual townsite of Union Bay, with its hotels, stores, bank and homes of those employed in the machine shops, ovens and yards, grew up across the highway, for many years nothing but a deeply-rutted wagon track. Initially there was little more than the "crudest beginning of a settlement. The forest grew to the water's edge, and a trail winding through the woods was the only means of communication. An Indian village stood at the mouth of Washer Creek. . . ."

Construction of the port, where Washer Creek empties into Baynes Sound, began in 1889; the rails and track were laid to Cumberland in April of the same year. Soon the mines at Cumberland were yielding tons of rich black Comox coal which acquired a reputation as the finest steam coal available on the west coast of North America. Before long the Dunsmuir family had its own fleet of colliers which operated between Union Bay and San Francisco, supplying the lucrative California market. The Dunsmuirs retained control of the massive operation until 1910, when it sold out to Canadian Collieries

Limited. Two years later the Canadian Collieries harnessed Puntledge River to supply electrical power to the whole Comox Valley. During both world wars Cumberland coal shipped through Union Bay made an important contribution to the allied cause by providing much of the fuel which powered the freighters rushing war material to Europe. At the time of demolition, the historic port was owned by Weldwood of Canada Limited.

In the years immediately preceding the First World War the port boomed and Cumberland's population soared to more than 13,000. Three thousand of these residents were Chinese. One interesting reminiscence of their contribution to the local economy was recalled by a Cumberland resident during that community's Diamond Jubilee, in 1973. On Sundays, he said, both the Union Steamships and Canadian Pacific boats called at Union Bay to unload freight, provisions, express, mail and passengers for Cumberland. Usually four or five boxcars handled the load, except in February when, in anticipation of the Chinese New Year, six and sometimes more cars were needed to haul the extra freight.

A former teamster recalled the days when he used to make a weekly trip between Parksville and Union Bay with supplies, much of them in liquid form, for labourers working on construction of the Canadian Pacific Railway. Today this run by modern paved highway takes about an hour; 70 years ago it took two days by horse-team through virgin forest. For mile after mile, other than the occasional railway work camp, he saw little more than deer and cougar on the trail. But, once he approached Union Bay, he knew he was back in civilization as the port was booming, with ships of all sizes and nationalities calling for coal. Upon unloading the last of his supplies he would spend the night in one of the hotels, before heading southward. Nights in Union Bay, he chuckled, had been anything but peaceful, with the local miners and dock workers boisterously mingling with seamen from all ports of the world.

Those days have gone forever. But for modern homes, a post office and store, and clearings where buildings obviously stood, Union Bay is but a shadow of its former self. Until recently, however, one of her original landmarks had survived, although in semi-demolished condition: the Royal Bank of Canada.

It was in March of 1966 that, prompted by news reports of the impending demolition, we defied a late season snowfall and paid a visit to Union Bay before the wreckers' hammers and crowbars completed their work of destruction. Packing camera gear and lunches into the car we headed north into a blizzard, only to have the weatherman change his mind within 30 miles and bless us, for the rest of the day, with glorious sunshine and shirtsleeve warmth.

Finally arriving at Union Bay, we had the place to ourselves — almost. For the wrecking crew was at work even then; nails groaned and reluctant boards screamed in protest as, board by board, nail by nail, the historic coal depot bowed to progress.

The wharf was undoubtedly the largest we had ever seen. From the bay it ran for an awesome distance toward, then parallel to, the highway. Because of its double function as dock and railway trestle, it must have been one of the longest on the Island. Boxcars could be shunted right out to the yawning bunkers and holds of ocean-going ships in days gone by. Although the enormous structure was still intact, its rails had been removed for scrap. Since then its thousands of beams,

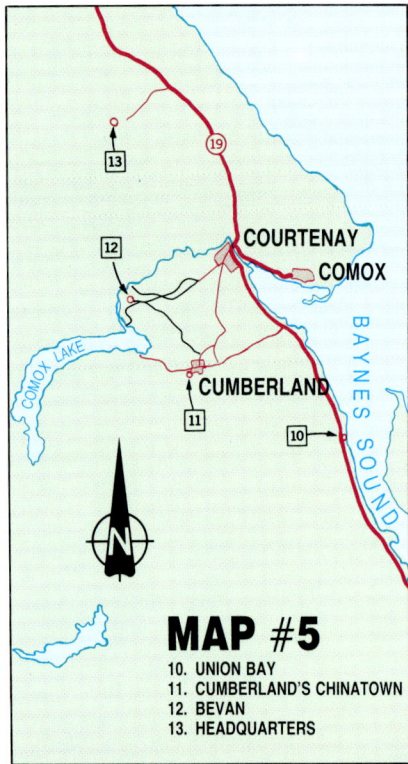

MAP #5

10. UNION BAY
11. CUMBERLAND'S CHINATOWN
12. BEVAN
13. HEADQUARTERS

(Above) Construction of the coke ovens at Union Bay.
(Below) Some of the remaining concrete ruins of what was once part of the shipping wharves at Union Bay. The largest is a hollow concrete tank with a large pipe attached.

(Left) W.E. Losee and his crew at Union Bay in 1888. These men built the first 50 ore cars in B.C. for the Union Colliery.
(Below left) Henry Wagner, alias "The Flying Dutchman."
(Below right) What remains of the town of Union Bay can be seen in the distance, across the Island Highway.
(Bottom left) A small creek is still directed by two solidly-built retaining walls.
(Bottom right) Numerous concrete ruins can yet be found in the trees at Union Bay.

thick as a man's waist and well preserved, have been salvaged also.

Upon climbing a rickety stairway to the trestle we were treated to an inspiring sight. The jade-green waters of Union Bay were perfectly still. Off to port a tug inched past Denman Island's northern tip with her tow of log booms; to starboard, a cement truck stormed along the highway. Even it did not awaken the sleepy village: a store, service station and homes resting on the roadside.

Most prominent feature of the dock was a rotting water tower which dated back to the romantic days of steam railroading. Since it had seen its last service long before Union Bay retired it was in much poorer condition than the trestle and only our expedition's youngest, lightest member dared its rickety ladder for a better view.

Where the trestle began were the remains of several structures which appeared to have been torn down some time before. Only broken concrete foundations and weathered scraps of timber were left. Here, too, although the trestle was quite high, trees had poked their heads through its beams; an indication of just how long it had been out of service.

After lunch on the beach we turned our attention to the most historic of Union Bay's ruins, its coke ovens. These two enormous structures of brick, each containing double rows of 50 ovens, dated back to Union Bay's earliest days. In 1966 they were overgrown with trees, one of which must have been at least 70 feet tall.

Assuming that their fires were stoked 24 hours daily, and even if one man could supervise several at a time, the 200 furnaces must have employed a large crew. (A hoe and a rake used in these ovens are in the Cumberland museum, where their length, and weight, draw considerable attention and comment.) Built of thousands of bricks — today highly prized as a rustic touch to new homes — they clearly indicated the importance that Union Bay had known in its heyday.

As previously mentioned, the actual kilns were shaped like beehives, with a hole in the roof for a chimney. Several had crumbled since being abandoned decades before, but most seemed to be in excellent condition. The main fuel of smelters, coke, is manufactured by heating coal to remove the natural gases, which allows it to burn "with much heat and little smoke." It is this quality of coke which has contributed to a renewed interest in coal in recent years.

A spur of the railway once ran between the two rows of ovens. But it too was a ghost of the past, its former bed sprouting trees and brambles. Here and there in the undergrowth and rubble, pieces of red pipe poked through the tangle like periscopes. These were the old fire hydrants. Scrap collectors had stripped them of their brass fittings.

Behind the kilns were the company buildings. The wreckers, who apparently did not stop for lunch, were working on the largest, one of the old machine shops where the company's rolling stock had been maintained. There were several other buildings the demolition crew had not yet touched, including the powerhouse, stores shed and offices. All showed their neglect, vandals having smashed the windows, but they appeared to be quite sturdy. Strangely, the powerhouse was still in operation.

Aside from much rubble the buildings were empty, except for an office, which still contained a large and expensive set of scales in a booth. Broken glass was everywhere.

At the townsite, one of the last visible survivors of Union Bay's forgotten glory was the old Fraser & Bishop general

store and post office. It was there that, one dark and stormy night, the notorious "Flying Dutchman" came to call — and a policeman died.

Abandoned and boarded up, the store stood alone with its memories, half surrounded by junk and abandoned cars. Perhaps its most intriguing feature, to treasure hunters at any rate, was its decrepit front porch. Just think of all those miners and sailors who tramped these stairs, money jingling in their pockets! At least, such was one visitor's theory. A hands-and-knees inspection of the rubble beneath the landing yielded nothing more than a broken beer bottle, dirty hands and a stiff neck. In the parking lot next door a young treasure hunter tried his luck with a metal detector, and soon uncovered a silver plated spoon. It was in excellent condition and a fine keepsake of old Union Bay.

The author had to content himself with a few photographs, a last look around and a trip to the files to re-acquaint himself with Henry Wagner — badman of the Old West, pirate, murderer and Flying Dutchman.

Once he had ridden with Butch Cassidy and the "Wild Bunch" — or so he claimed. But it was his penchant for robbing coastal communities by motorboat that made Wagner's flamboyant title (an erroneous one at that, as he was of German descent) known to British Columbia police as "one of the most notorious criminals who have infested the waters of Puget Sound and the Gulf of Georgia in many years." Time and again in the early months of 1913, Wagner and his accomplice Bill Julian struck isolated ports with lightning speed and efficiency, to make their getaway in a fast motorboat. Operating out of Lasqueti Island, the pair ranged far and wide. Among their targets was Union Bay, after which they had sped off into the night.

Chief Const. David Stephenson, the British Columbia Provincial Police officer in charge of the northern half of Vancouver Island, knew that, sooner or later, the pirates would go to the well once too often. The question was, where — and when? His jurisdiction added up to something like 8,000 square miles. Yet the veteran officer was convinced that the pirates would return to Union Bay, where Fraser & Bishop's store was a tempting target. Situated only a few hundred feet from the docks, it was an easy and an inviting prize. And it was there that Stephenson stationed two of his men, rookies Harry Westaway and Gordon Ross.

For night after night the two men stood watch in the shadows, waiting for the seaborne phantoms to strike. But morning would come without a visit, and news that they had struck elsewhere. On the rainy morning of March 3, 1913, the constables resumed their vigil from the shelter of a tree. All was still as the town slept. Suddenly one of them spotted a faint glow inside the store: a flashlight. They moved stealthily towards the store. Having decided to enter by way of the post office, for which they had been issued a key, they cautiously unlocked the door and slipped inside. As just Westaway was armed, Ross carrying only a nightstick and a flashlight, the former took the lead.

Tiptoeing through the darkened post office, a gabled addition to the left of the two-storey structure, they came to the door leading into the store. Ross jerked the handle, flipped the switch of his flashlight, and stepped through the doorway and to one side to permit Westaway to cover the room with his gun.

No sooner had Ross aimed his light than he saw two men crouched behind the counter. Ross lunged forward, but he had not taken more than a step when there was an explosion as the first burglar fired his Colt revolver. The .44 slug passed right through Ross' shoulder and buried itself in Westaway's side.

As Westaway fell, unconscious, to the floor the second burglar made a run for the door — leaving a wounded Ross alone with the murderous gunman. Before the assailant could fire again, the heroic young officer closed the distance between them. By this time his flashlight had gone flying and the store was again plunged into total darkness. When he crashed into the invisible robber he slashed wildly with his fist and nightstick, and tried frantically to get the other's gun.

His opponent fought back wildly, and struggled time and again to use his Colt, only to find the officer's steely grip, despite his wound, to be too great. Back and forth they grappled and cursed, and flailed about with gun, club and fist.

Their duel has been described by former assistant commissioner of provincial police Cecil Clark as "one of the greatest man-to-man battles in western police history. . . .

"Both men were powerfully built, and to each it was a life and death struggle. The policeman knew the armed robber meant murder, and the desperado, thinking the policeman armed, knew he would use his gun if he could reach it."

Finally it was over. Although seriously wounded and weakened by loss of blood, and matched against an opponent who was both powerful and desperate, Constable Ross had succeeded in "equalizing" the burglar's Colt with his sturdy nightstick — almost breaking it over the man's head. Only then had his opponent collapsed to the floor, enabling Ross to handcuff him.

Moments later, when help reached the scene, Ross was blinded by blood and ready to pass out. Constable Westaway still lay motionless where he had fallen, in a growing pool of blood. Then the Flying Dutchman, who was battered almost beyond recognition, was led away and formally charged with having murdered a policeman.

On the morning of August 28, 1913, Henry Wagner, alias Ferguson and the Flying Dutchman — whisky smuggler, pirate and general bad man — paid the supreme penalty for the last and greatest of his many sins. Characteristically, he maintained his "reputation for nerve and coolness" to the end, it being reported that he strode to the scaffold and leaped up the steps without assistance or the slightest sign of nervousness.

Today, all that remains of the commodious wharves at Union Bay are a few rotting timbers and some enormous chunks of concrete. The remains of some coke ovens can yet be found, although most are overgrown and forgotten. Hidden in the trees are the concrete ruins of long abandoned buildings. In the area where offices and buildings once stood, huge mounds of coal slag, a favourite with dirt bikers, is all that remains of the once busy shipping terminal that stood on the site. Across the small bay where visitors probe for Manilla clams, the small settlement of Union Bay reposes quietly alongside the Island Highway. ♣

(Above) Bunkers at Union Bay under construction. Robert Dunsmuir chose Union Bay as a shipping terminal because Royston, although closer to the Cumberland mines, was too shallow for the ships which would call from around the globe for coal. (Below) Construction of Union Bay's coke ovens, two enormous structures of brick, each containing double rows of 50 beehive ovens which, when completed, operated around the clock.

Cumberland's Chinatown

IT was in 1869 that Sam Cliffe, a Nanaimo miner, first heard of black outcroppings in the Comox Valley. Sure that his Indian informant had described seams of coal, Cliffe called together 10 of his friends. At that time the government offered 100 acres of coal land for every $1,000 invested in its development and, after pooling their resources, the fledgling syndicate hired the native as guide, canoed up the Courtenay River and hiked overland to Comox Lake. On the shale banks of what was to become Coal Creek, the party staked its claims.

Making the future site of nearby Royston their base, Cliffe and his partners hacked a trail to the creek and began the arduous task of grading a railway bed through the forest. However, despite the obvious potential of their claims, the enterprising partners of the Union Coal Mining Company exhausted their own limited funds and could not raise sufficient capital to continue construction. Consequently they sold out to coal baron Robert Dunsmuir, then active at Wellington, who had been watching their efforts with interest. Five months after he began operations, on July 25, 1888, Dunsmuir incorporated the Union Colliery Company of British Columbia Limited. In the following decades Comox coal would become known and used around the globe.

The frustrated Sam Cliffe lived just long enough to see the mines he had staked enter production.

Among Dunsmuir's initial priorities was a sawmill, and he commissioned the logging firm of Grant and Mounce to begin work. Several years ago 83-year-old Royston resident Charley Grant recalled how his father had moved the heavy mill engine, built by the Albion Ironworks in Victoria, into Union. When the side-wheel steamer *Barbara Boscowitz* landed the engine on the beach at Royston, the loggers had faced a herculean task in getting it through the bush to Union. As the road to the new mine site had been cleared for just a mile and a half, they were forced to cut trees and haul them out of the way with their team of oxen — a job which took them three months. Once the little mill was in production, Mr. Grant said, he had gone to work (at the age of nine) as a teamster, hauling rails by horse-team up the future right of way to the mines.

Sam Cliffe and his partners had originally planned to build their railroad to tidewater at Royston. However, Dunsmuir realized that this harbour was too shallow for his needs and diverted the railroad to the deep-water port of Union Bay.

One of the ill-fated Union Company partners, John Dick, originally arrived in the Comox Valley on behalf of an English syndicate which had an interest in a coal seam on the Tsable River. They too had attempted to construct a railway to tide-

(Above left) Coal baron Robert Dunsmuir.
(Above right) Now the last remaining building in Chinatown, this log cabin was once the office of Robert Dunsmuir.
(Opposite page) Cumberland in the beginning. Originally called the "Camp" by residents, it was christened Union, then Cumberland. These homes for employees were built when Robert Dunsmuir bought out Sam Cliffe. The locomotive is the "Queen Anne." (Inset) Although newly painted and renovated, these homes are remainders of Cumberland's coal era.
(Below) This painting by artist Bill Maximick depicts Cumberland's Dunsmuir Avenue c1906.

water, but when they ran out of money, Dick switched his allegiance to the Union Company. Under Dunsmuir, Dick supervised construction of the railway grade from Coal Creek to Royston, started work on Nos. 2 and 3 shafts, and commenced the slope to No. 4.

The town of "Union" sprang into existence. In 1897 it was incorporated as the City of Cumberland, after the English county of that name. Within two years its population had soared to more than 1,000 whites and 3,000 Chinese and Japanese, all of whom had been imported by the company. Chinatown, constructed on the edge of a swamp about a mile west of Cumberland proper, became a thriving, bustling city unto itself. In its heyday it was only second in size to that of San Francisco, and boasted about 100 business establishments, including 24 groceries, five drugstores, five tailor shops, five butcher shops, five tobacco shops, four barber shops, four restaurants, three hand laundries, two shoe shops, two hardware stores, and several herbalists.

There were also a dentist, a photographer and a watch repair shop. In the way of recreation there were two 400-seat theatres, 100 fan tan houses, eight lottery houses, two judo athletic clubs, a fortune teller and an unknown number of opium dens.

In the world of education there were three separate classrooms, rather than schools, each with from 15 to 20 pupils, who learned the three R's; 'rithmetic with the help of the time-proven abacus.

Besides the Chinese temples there was a single Christian church, under the guidance of Rev. Mah Sang.

Walking along the crowded main thoroughfares of Chinatown, Shanghai and Chang, "was like going down a street in Hong Kong," John Brown, one of the last of Cumberland's original inhabitants recalled in 1957. He said a "good" Chinese earned $1.50 a day and a poor worker 75¢ a day. "But they got everything else free — water, light, oil, lamps and land on which to build their own shacks. There were no deductions, so that many Chinese became quite well-to-do and sent money back to Canton to relatives there."

Last of Cumberland's 40-member Negro community, "Coon Town," John Brown was also one of its most intriguing characters. The spry old miner had thought nothing of packing alone into the dreaded Pitt River country, deep in the forbidding hills behind New Westminster, until a broken kneecap had finally slowed him down — at the age of 86. Since his arrival in British Columbia, 70 years before, he had worked in the coal mines in winter months and packed off into the mountains each and every summer. He could remember Cumberland's Chinatown at the height of its glory.

Another long-time resident was Mrs. Laura Little, who remembered the time when "Fan tan games ran 23 hours a day, Grant and Mounce hauled logs down the main street by bull team to the mill at the edge of town, you reached the hospital by following a footpath through the woods."

Medically, Chinese took care of their own; the fan tan houses also provided free meals to the aged and needy, and doubled as meeting houses without charge.

But all that is past. Until recent years a handful of elderly residents could recall the days when the Benevolent Association ran Chinatown without recourse to Canadian law — until the notorious "tong war" came to Cumberland and brought violence, intrigue and the provincial police in its wake.

Until this grim development the association had done an admirable job in a unique way. Two merchants from each street would be elected annually to act as overseers of day to day business matters. In times of emergency, the association would call a town meeting at which all merchants were expected to attend, when the matter would be resolved by discussion and vote. Business transactions bearing the committee's seal were considered to be legal and binding. But for the tong war which later erupted between the Free Masons and National League Party, this system seems to have worked well.

Cumberland has known death by fire and mine explosion over the years. One of the worst underground blasts claimed 30 of the hardy Asian miners, and prompted a steady migration to other areas. Then came the *coup de grace* by depression and oil.

In recent years only the mine at nearby Tsable River remained in production; now even it has shut down. The day when Cumberland pits produced a staggering 2,500 tons of coal each 24 hours is gone forever.

As early as 1963 the chamber of commerce had considered a plan to preserve what was left of Chinatown but the scheme failed to materialize. Then those in quest of salvage lumber and curios completed their work and Chinatown belongs to the ages.

Nevertheless bottle and curio collectors continue to call from around the province and from many American states, although the incredible boom of the late '60s has slowed to a trickle. There is little for them to see now; certainly nothing to give the slightest indication of Cumberland's former glory.

Most imposing of Chinatown's ruins which had survived to the very end was the two-storey Lum Yung Club. Although empty, it had afforded hours of intriguing exploration to visitors. What furniture was left had been smashed by vandals and all windows were broken. The rear of the building had been sinking into the swamp despite an attempt to slow the inevitable with cordwood pilings.

Shreds of dirty paper, covered with enigmatic Chinese symbols, littered the earthen basement amid broken glass, furniture and cobwebs. A back room off the main floor contained several overturned, single-construction benches and desks. Each desk had been lined with locking drawers. Likely this had been part of the casino. The top floor, we were told, had been a shrine.

Even the landscape has changed beyond recognition, the swamp steadily encroaching on the former townsite which, in recent years, had resembled a First World War battlefield, complete with trenches, "shell holes," mounds of black soil and clay, and rubble. Today, where bottle collectors laboured so hard under a hot sun, fireweed and couch grass reign.

Almost to the end, four of Chinatown's original inhabitants continued to live in their crumbling, rent-free shacks, content to end their days in the homes they had known so long. With each passing the bulldozers had claimed another victim.

These pioneers were reserved and, beyond a shy wave and a smile, avoided visitors. During summer they would sit in the sun and talk, perhaps of the golden days when the Dunsmuir mines roared around the clock.

"When the mines were open," said one, "there were so many people and buildings you couldn't see a tree or blade of grass. There were three shifts a day — but you hadn't time to see the sky."

A tattered bulletin board behind the "evening bench" was an itemized accounting of the costs of maintaining the graves of their comrades who had passed on. The survivors shared equally the cost of keeping their little cemetery weeded and the fence painted. As each year passed, more and more joined their ancestors, a fact which raised the share of those surviving. But none complained.

The youngest of these pioneers was a distinguished, grey-haired gentleman who had been in Cumberland for 40 years. He would walk among the tourists, picking up discarded soft drink and beer bottles as he regaled them with tales of the time when the town held more than old men and ghosts.

Today visitors find it hard to believe that this ghost town once boasted 3,000 inhabitants, that its crowded streets had been compared to those of Hong Kong. At one point the old townsite was leased by its owners, Weldwood of Canada, to a private operator who charged bottle collectors a daily fee to dig.

When provincial museum officials learned of this commercialization and expressed their concern, Chinatown sparked considerable comment in newspapers and on radio. Said a museum spokesman: "We are being plain stupid. We have allowed this to happen when, in the United States, such a site would be fully protected. . . . It's stupid, it's wasteful."

In his defence the businessman who had leased the property said that he had tried, three years before, "to interest the people around here in saving what was left of the town and restoring it, but they took no action. There were others who laughed at the idea of preserving the place."

Weldwood reportedly had offered the land to the village of Cumberland for an honorarium if citizens would make an effort to save Chinatown.

In the meantime, Canadian and American visitors continued to haul away thousands of bottles; it is local lore that two American dealers trucked almost 300,000 bottles across the border, for sale at an average price of $1.25 each.

Of particular interest to local historians was an ancient log cabin. Then occupied by one of the surviving Chinese, known as Jumbo, it was the original office of coal magnate Robert Dunsmuir and, according to legend, served for a time as the local lock-up. Weldwood had voiced plans to reassemble the cabin, built in 1869, in Vancouver as part of a mining museum.

More recently, the Cumberland chamber of commerce considered moving the cabin to the vacant lot alongside the museum, on Dunsmuir Avenue. This was not done, and today, it remains in Chinatown, having achieved the distinction of being the first structure erected in Chinatown and the last to survive.

Later the Chinatown lease changed hands and the late Lawrence Schendl, who had worked in the mines and well remembered when coal reigned supreme in Comox Valley, was made caretaker of the site. In later years his interest, as had so many others, turned to the coveted "tiger" whisky jugs, so-called opium bottles, fan tan chips and jewellery uncovered by the thousands. As recently as 1967, he said, the townsite was literally paved with discarded glassware and Oriental pottery, although several pioneer collectors had made forays into the area.

Then had come an American dealer, who hauled bottles away by the truckload. Others followed and word swept the Pacific Northwest, and beyond, of the bonanza waiting at Cumberland. During the next four years thousands tried their luck in Chinatown. Few left empty-handed.

An untold number of the intriguing collector's items must remain yet, buried deep in the swampy earth. But visitors have to work hard for their treasure now, as Mr. Schendl

(whose chickens unearthed thousands of bottles in his own backyard) had warned with a grin. Today's treasure hunters come to look around and to wonder at Chinatown's mysteries. Few get to dig for whatever artifacts may remain.

Fortunately for posterity, some of Cumberland's, and of Chinatown's, memories will survive, thanks to the establishment of a small museum by the chamber of commerce. Because of the chamber's efforts a valuable collection of relics, many of them related to the mines, has been gathered and placed on display.

Cumberland, when incorporated under that name as a city in 1897, could boast of being "the smallest and westernmost city in North America with a population of 3,000." But when changing fortunes meant a decline in population, from a high of 13,000, the community, which celebrated its Diamond Jubilee in 1973, reverted to a village status in 1958.

According to a booklet prepared by the chamber of commerce: "Incorporation as a city spurred farm development in both the Minto and Comox areas of the valley and farmers were soon paying regular visits to sell their dairy products, their fruits and vegetables and eggs to the thriving community based on the coal mines." Over the years, when the mines were shut down periodically as the result of labour strife, the friendly bond between the communities of Cumberland and Courtenay was affirmed by the fact that the latter centre, predominantly agricultural, supplied the striking miners with eggs, butter and vegetables for as long as six months on "tick."

Now a residential community, Cumberland has lost many of its better-known landmarks in recent years. As mentioned, Chinatown has followed its cruelly named contemporaries, Coontown and Japtown, into oblivion. In the village itself, even the architecturally striking employees' social hall has fallen victim to "progress."

Another recent victim is Cumberland Hospital, the third oldest on Vancouver Island. When the original structure was built in 1895, it was called the Union and Comox District Hospital. Later two wards were added. Nurses, according to the records, earned from $5 to $10 dollars a day in 1902. When poetess Pauline Johnson came to town, three-quarters of a century ago, she gave two widely attended readings at the hospital, the coal company even scheduling a special train so as to enable settlers from throughout the valley to attend.

NOS. 1, 2, 3. . .

These early tunnels, first to tap what was to become internationally famous as the Comox seam, never did become big producers. No. 1, opened in 1889, and a thousand feet deep, was located behind No. 1 Japtown, one and a half miles west of town on the road to Comox Lake. For many years ore dumps marked the site.

No. 2 Slope was started behind Chinatown when No. 1 "did not lend itself to large scale development." It too was short-lived, amounting to little more than a prospect. Soon work was begun on No. 3, which was driven into the hills south of "Camp" (Union). Like Nos. 1 and 2, No. 3 did not see a productive career.

It remained for No. 4 mine to put Cumberland on the map as a coal town. Situated on the "Lake shore" slope, beside Comox Lake, it soon became one of the largest mines on the Pacific Coast and remained in operation from 1888 to 1935 — half a century. No. 4 also gained something of a reputation as a killer after two explosions, in 1922 and 1923, killed 51 men (17 whites, 28 Chinese and 6 Japanese).

Old John Brown remembered No. 4 — and the time that an

(Above) Cumberland's Chinatown at the turn of the century. Walking along its main thoroughfares, Shanghai and Chang, was said to be "like going down a street in Hong Kong" when 3,000 persons lived there.
(Below left) The Lum Yung Club in Chinatown shortly before demolition.
(Below right) The grave of Low Hock Shun, 1861-1948, in the Chinese cemetery.

explosion killed so many of his workmates. In those days, he said, the miners kept a canary in a cage to warn them against a lethal build-up of gas. When the canary fell off its perch it was time to get out. On this terrible day the canary keeled over and the men began a mad scramble for the surface. Those working in John Brown's slope made it to the pithead; many more did not. "At the pithead," he said, "the dead men were laid out in rows, like the fingers on your hand."

Fortunately for three of the "dead" — Bobby Brown, Johnny Webber and Jimmy Gibbs — they were revived by artificial respiration. The others were interred in the crowded Cumberland cemeteries (white, Chinese and Japanese), among their comrades who had died in other accidents, in other pits. This was the way of coal mining.

No. 5, a "shaft" mine located a mile northwest of Cumberland, was started in 1895 and worked until 1947, although it was closed for a total of six of those years "for various reasons." Almost 600 feet deep, it was known, among other things, for its stables at the base of the pit for the mules which spent their working lifetimes underground.

No. 6 mine was situated directly behind the present municipal office and was in operation from 1898 until 1931; 614 feet deep, the shaft continued to be used to pump water from No. 5 after work in No. 6 was discontinued (both mines, in later years, being connected). Cumberland's worst mining disaster occurred here, on February 15, 1901, when an explosion claimed 64 lives. No. 6 was abandoned and sealed in 1931. Today, not so much as a plaque marks the spot — just a large slab of concrete in the undergrowth. Even with directions it takes several minutes to locate the site. It would seem proper that some form of recognition be made here. ♣

Bevan

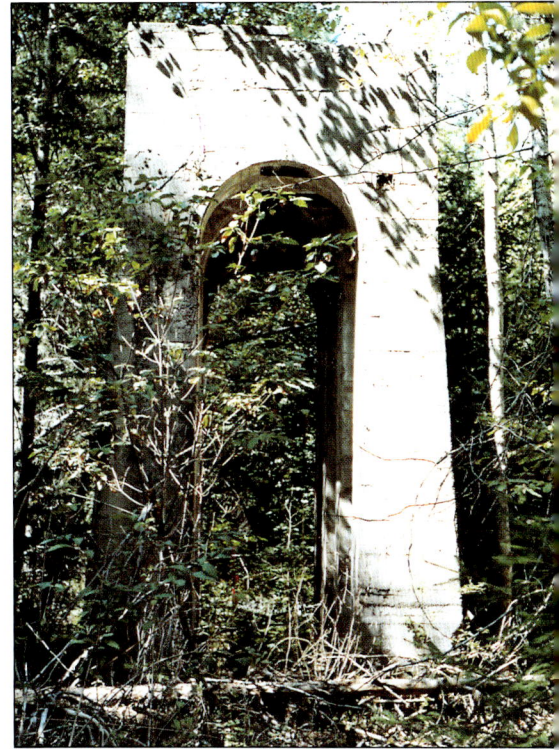

(Above) The Power House of No. 8 mine on the Puntledge River at Bevan.
(Right) Concrete ruins of main mine buildings of No. 8 mine, Bevan.
(Below) The Puntledge River near Bevan.

FOUR miles to the north of Cumberland, the satellite community of Bevan came into being as the result of No. 7 mine, which entered operation in 1902. In 1911, 50 houses, a large store, school and hotel (Bevan Lodge) were erected here. Only 10 years later, Bevan was dying. Most of its fine homes were moved to a section of Cumberland known as Townsite. The rest, including a fair-sized Chinatown, were razed; only the hotel survived. Today it is a provincial home for the mentally handicapped.

No. 8 was a shaft mine at Puntledge, between Bevan and Courtenay on the Lake Trail, some two miles from Bevan. Here, two shafts, each 1,000 feet deep, were sunk. Between 1912 and 1914 all-steel surface installations of "the very latest" design were erected at the pithead. However, after very little exploration around the shaft bottoms, work was discontinued and the shafts allowed to flood. Not until 1936 was No. 8 reactivated, the barren years of 1914-36 being known locally as the "million dollar mystery." When the mine finally did become an active producer it was too late, history had passed it by. The increasing popularity of oil and gas, and discovery of the Leduc coalfields in Alberta spelled *finis* for deep thin-seam mining and No. 8. In February, 1953, the mine was closed for good. Only the remains of some concrete buildings and ore dumps survive.

During the summer of 1973 an attempt to burn garbage in the ore dump of old No. 8 started a fire which, upon its taking firm hold in the waste coal, was feared would burn for at least two years. Here, over an area of 35 acres, more than 1.5 million cubic yards of coal waste had been dumped. Firefighters could

(Left) The hoist and tipple of No. 8 mine, Bevan. Here, between 1912-14, two 1,000-foot shafts were sunk and ultra-modern equipment installed at the pithead. Then exploratory work was halted and the shafts allowed to flood. In 1936 No. 8 was reactivated and became a good producer until permanently closed in 1953. The inactive years of 1914-36 are still referred to locally as the "million dollar mystery."

not use water on the fire "because it just supplies more oxygen and helps the fire burn," explained a spokesman for Weldwood of Canada. "At the beginning we put about 1,000 gallons of water on the burning pile and when it got about six feet under it formed steam and exploded. We will just have to close the area off and let it burn."

With fall rains, he warned, "it will stink up the countryside and people will be complaining. The pile has very heavy sulphur contents. At night you can see the white and blue flames burning off."

This incident, one of many which had plagued Weldwood in recent years, was said to be the last straw; the company finally closed off access to the historic coal mining area.

A similar fire, in wastes from the old Tsable River mine, some 16 miles north of Courtenay, had been burning for more than 10 years. The noxious smell of the burning sulphur at Bevan, said the Weldwood spokesman, was a poignant reminder of the mining days when "all the people used to burn coal and you could never keep paint on your house for more than 18 months."

The Tsable River operation was coal mining's last gasp in the Comox Valley. During the 1940s only No. 8 mine at Bevan had remained in operation besides the younger-generation Tsable River shafts (the only one of the mines in the valley which had not been designated by number). Twenty miles from Cumberland, and four miles west of Buckley Bay, the Tsable River workings were begun as a prospect in 1945; a more permanent tipple and pithead buildings being built four years after. Three times daily dozens of miners would board

buses in Cumberland for the drive to Tsable River which, in 1948, was rated by some as being "a big seam. Goes 12 to 14 feet wide in spots, and mostly it's a clear nine feet of clean coal. No rock or sulphur between."

Although some outsiders had suggested that Cumberland was on its way to becoming a ghost town, most residents heatedly denied this and expressed confidence that the town would never die — "not while there's coal in the hills."

Because Canadian Collieries had promised residents that it would not encourage settlement at Tsable River. Cumberland residents thought the newer operation to be "the biggest insurance we have. . . . There's enough (coal) to last a hundred years, and then some," they said.

But, 18 years later, Tsable River — the "last mine of the Cumberland coal saga" — and known as the mine that wouldn't die — faded into oblivion like all the others before it. After Canadian Collieries Limited ceased production in 1960, a local syndicate assumed control of the operation on a smaller scale and continued to mine coal until November, 1966. Then the mine shut down permanently, the portal was sealed off and the machinery removed. When the last operating coal mine on Vancouver Island lost its biggest contract, to supply a government steam plant on the lower mainland, it was over.

Most of its employees were over the age of 55 and had worked in the mines since their teens. Mourned Sid Eccleston, who started work underground at the age of 14: ". . .A lot of people say they (would) never go down a mine. But if you've done it all your life. . . . A mine isn't just a black hole in the ground. You get to like working down there."   ♣

Headquarters

THE cost of real estate, as everyone knows, has soared beyond the reach of many Canadians, who wistfully recall the pre-inflationary '50s and '60s when comfortable, reasonably low-cost housing was within the reach of most working people.

Just how cheaply houses could be bought was demonstrated at Headquarters, north of Courtenay, in the summer of 1958. In a single two line paragraph it was announced that the company town of Headquarters was to be placed on the block, its homes sold for one dollar each. These were not shanties, but "fine, weather-proof houses." The catch was that they had to be moved from the Comox Logging and Railway Company townsite, beside the Tsolum River, within a specified time. Even the two-storey school house had to go. . . .

Headquarters, at the north end of the Comox Valley, was the creation of Gen. A.D. McRae, for many years one of the principals of the Canadian Western Lumber Company. In 1911, on the banks of the Tsolum River, he selected the site for the company town. Before long Headquarters consisted of 30-odd homes, a school, general store, hotel, dance hall, maintenance shops for the company's logging and railway equipment, and sawmill. The town's name was suggested by the fact that the company offices were located here.

Headquarters served as the capital of a private empire, the company owning a timber tract of 80,000 acres, linked in the beginning by 44 miles of railway, five locomotives, 150 cars, a force of 500 men (this included mainland employees), and a fleet of four tugboats and a river steamer.

Originally the Comox Logging and Railway Company shipped its hemlock logs to Royston by train, then towed them, in booms, to mills on the lower mainland. Early in 1914, notes Campbell River photographer-author Peggy Young, the company decided that, because hemlock waterlogs rapidly, and they were losing a high percentage of their logs, it would be cheaper to mill them on the site. Thus work was begun on a sawmill at Headquarters.

From England came all the necessary equipment for a sawmill which was built to last of concrete. All went according to plan and the mill was ready to cut its first log when the First World War started and Headquarters, like many other logging operations, suspended operations.

This is one explanation for the fact that General McRae's expensive sawmill at Headquarters never cut a board. A second version is quite the opposite. Ben Hughes, writing in the *Colonist* in 1958, notes that the Comox Company built the mill, then discovered that it would be cheaper to saw the logs at Fraser River mills. As a result the sawmill at Headquarters was dismantled and the village doomed to become nothing more than a small logging community.

As such it survived for 40 years, by which time the logging railways had long yielded to trucks.

Unofficial mayor for all of those years was Bob Filberg, company superintendent, who, although he became a millionaire, never lost touch with his employees, many of whom were grateful to him for having devised ways to keep them

Ruins of the sawmill at Headquarters today.

working during the leaner years.

Another noteworthy Headquarters resident was Major Hilton, manager, who, with his wife, occupied the first house in the town.

The Filberg home consisted of four stories, had 50 windows and hardwood floors. In 1958 40-year company employee Joe Bergsma bought it for one dollar.

Headquarters had survived the loss of its sawmill, the phasing out of railway logging, and the first years of trucking. But this newcomer made it possible for logging operations to be centralized at Duncan Bay. And with that decision the company houses, school and shops were sold for removal. Only the gaunt concrete ruin of the sawmill remains, between river and country crossroads, in a swamp of alders.   ♣

Fort Rupert

Fort Rupert is the newest and best built station of the Hudson Bay Company I have seen, and the gardens are very nicely laid out. Of course, like all the rest, it is stockaded, and has its gallery and bastions. It stands almost in the middle of the Indian village. Some idea of the number of salmon in these parts, and of the prodigality of the Hudson Bay Company under the old regime may be gathered from the fact told me by one of these officers, that before he took charge of the post, 3000 salmon were used annually as manure for the garden.

☆   ☆   ☆

A century and a quarter after Comdr. R.C. Mayne, R.N., F.R.G.S., penned these lines for his memoirs, *Four years in British Columbia and Vancouver Island,* Fort Rupert of the attractive — and richly fertilized gardens — is history. Only a single, towering chimney of stone survives of this historic outpost. But its memories of the first coal mining on Vancouver Island — and of its infamous "massacre" — remain.

As in the establishment of other Vancouver Island communities, it was coal which first drew attention to the site of what was to become Fort Rupert, in 1835. It was not until another 14 years had passed that the Hudson's Bay Company (HBC) became interested enough in its mining potential to establish here. One of the reasons for the time lag is the fact that it was 1846 before the HBC found a prospective customer, the Pacific Mail Steamship Company, for its coal.

Ten years before, Dr. William Fraser Tolmie, a company physician stationed at Fort McLoughlin, had been told by an Indian of coal outcroppings on the northeastern tip of Van-

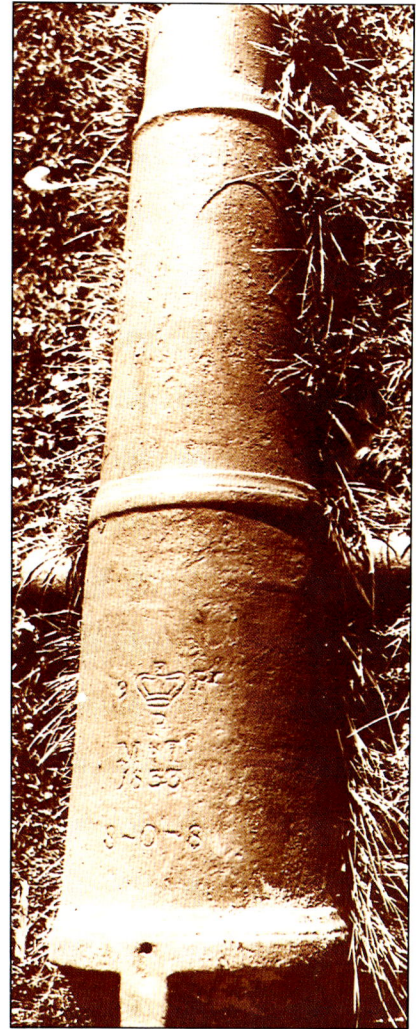

(Above) In 1873, Robert Hunt, factor for the Hudson's Bay Company at Fort Rupert, purchased the fort from his former employer.

(Opposite page, top) A totem pole at Fort Rupert in 1973.

(Opposite page, bottom) Clam digging on Storey Beach, Fort Rupert.

(Left) Capt. William Henry McNeill has been described as tough as nails, with a notorious temper.

Adm. George Henry Richards prevented all-out war between the Indians at Fort Rupert and Nanaimo.

George Blenkinsop, in charge of Fort Rupert during McNeill's absence, accused coal miners Andrew Muir and John McGregor of instigating a sit-down strike.

Gov. Richard Blanshard. He ordered Captain Wellesley to take Nawwittie village by force.

(Right) An old cannon at Fort Rupert.
(Below) Storey Beach, Fort Rupert.

couver Island. This report prompted a survey of the designated area by the venerable HBC steamer *Beaver,* and verification of the fact that there was, indeed coal there.

Further confirmation of the region's potential as a coal producer was provided by Commander Gordon, HMS *Cormorant,* who traded articles of clothing and assorted goods for 62 tons of coal in 1846. Payment amounted to four shillings a ton.

The HBC, having decided to abandon Fort McLoughlin, let the matter lie. Later, upon realizing that the closing of its Milbanke Sound outpost had been a mistake, the company decided that McLoughlin should be replaced, although not in its original location. Upon the formal settlement of the 49th parallel as the international boundary, and Admiralty interest in Vancouver Island coal, the choice of site resolved itself. In 1849 plans were complete for construction of a new "super" fortress to be known as Fort Rupert.

The man chosen to build the new post — intended to be one of the strongest fortifications west of the Rockies due to the neighbouring Nahwittie tribesmen's reputation as fierce warriors — was Capt. W.H. McNeill. As even a glance at the record shows, Captain McNeill was just the man for such a challenging job. Tough as nails, with a notorious temper, he earned the respect of white and red man as a courageous and industrious servant of the fur trading empire.

A strict disciplinarian, more than once McNeill's fiery temperament came to the fore. Even in his later years, toward the end of a long and active career as shipmaster, his blacking of a grocer's eye sent him to court to answer a charge of aggravated assault.

This could only be considered "small time" for a man who once flogged and stranded his steward, and whose iron rule had led to a mutiny aboard the historic steamship *Beaver.*

Prior to the start of construction of Fort Rupert, on the shore of Beaver Harbour, no Indians had settled there, although the site was long known to them as a safe harbour and a rich clamming ground. With the arrival of McNeill and company, members of the powerful Kwakiutl nation rushed to the vicinity to take advantage of the new trading post. Overnight, a "boom town" of cedar-planked long houses, named Ku-Kultz, appeared on the beach, and the lonely whites working within the fort's palisades found themselves deafened by "shrieks and cries, the beating of tribal drum; the noise of fighting and the unearthly yelling and rattling of medicine men. . . ." It was, to say the least, a terrifying orchestra, and the vastly outnumbered whites spent many a night lying awake and listening to the screeches, shouting and beat of the drums just a few hundred yards from Fort Rupert's picketed walls.

Between the few whites and hundreds of warriors stood a formidable 18-foot-high stockade, constructed of logs shipped from Alaska, and a network of bastions armed with cannon. Although all HBC forts were so constructed, Fort Rupert was something special — "the best fort the company ever built." Captain McNeill and his officers had taken every care to design and to construct an outpost that could be defended by a handful of employees against overwhelming numbers. The most impressive piece of architecture was the fort's main gate, great thought having been given to the building of a bastion which was positioned directly above the entranceway so as to overshadow all activity there. To ensure that unfriendly visitors were confined to the cannons' line of fire, the gate had been built with tall and sturdy palisades on either side, with further bastions positioned at each corner of the walls. In effect, this created a "tunnel" through which all vis-

itors to the fort had to pass in order to gain entry. Any frontal assault, in the yaw of the fort's cannon, would have been suicidal.

Life in the lonely outpost, if one gives credence to first-hand reports of visitors, was hardly a bed of roses for the HBC employees stationed there. One horrified caller, missionary Richard Dowson, wrote in April, 1859: "Fort Rupert is the H.B. Company's fort at the north end of the Island and consists of (a) wooden stockade about 18 feet high and 120 feet square built of strong thick posts sunk deeply in the ground. There is a gallery all round the inside about four feet from the top and two bastions at the opposite corners with a few guns in each. In the interior are a few wooden houses and the company's stores. The population consists of the H.B. Co's clerk in charge of the fort with his half-caste wife, and about a dozen European mechanics and laborers with the native women who are living with them. . . .

"Outside the fort is the Indian camp, a collection of wooden houses or rather huts with a population of about a thousand, including men, women and children. I think the Quackrolls (Kwakiutls) — the tribe about Fort Rupert — are the most bloodthirsty of all the Indian tribes on the Northwest Coast. When I was there there was (sic) plenty of heads and other human remains to be seen on the beach, and one body of a woman was found fastened to a tree partly in the water, and the lower part all eaten away by fish.

"A short time before my visit some of their canoes came in from a war expedition and landed a prisoner, when all the other Indians rushed down in a flood from their houses and ate the poor wretch alive close to the gate of the fort. The white people in the fort looked on from the gallery but could not do anything to stop the hideous scene."

Despite such horrors Dowson made a personal inspection of the sprawling camp, and reported the houses to be "the dirtiest I have yet been in. They are built much in the same way as all the other Indian houses I have seen, that is, four walls of posts and rough planks and a sloping roof of planks, with abundance of holes and crevices for the smoke to get out, and the wind and rain to get in. They are of fair size and height and each contain four or five families, or rather perhaps, branches of the same family, each squatted round its own particular fire which is simply a bundle of sticks lighted on the floor.

"Fort Rupert is rather a solitary position for the gentleman in charge of it. The nearest white settlement is Nanaimo between which and him are more than 200 miles of almost impenetrable bush and forest. His only communication with the outer world being the H.B. Co's. steamer's visits twice a year, however, he seems to bear his confinement cheerfully and certainly gave me a most kind and hearty welcome."

Others who called at Fort Rupert and the Beaver Harbour village carried away unpleasant memories. In the summer of 1860 Capt. George H. Richards, in command of Her Majesty's survey ship *Plumper,* and Comdr. W.A.R. Pearse, master of HMS *Alert,* toured the encampment. Richards reported to Adm. Sir Robert L. Baynes: ". . .The whole tribe, amounting to between 600 and 700 people, (live) in a most disgraceful condition." The HBC officer in charge of the fort, he said, had told him that the natives "had been in a state of intoxication ever since their return from Victoria some three weeks previously, from the effects of which they were only now recovering. Their conduct at times had been of so violent a character that Mr. Weynton (ranking HBC officer at Fort Rupert) with

(Above) Overnight, a "boom town" of cedar-planked longhouses appeared on the beach, and the lonely whites stationed at Fort Rupert found themselves deafened by "shrieks and cries, the beating of tribal drums, the noise of fighting and the unearthly yelling and rattling of medicine men."

(Right) Officers of HMS Scout and members of the Nahwittie tribe which settled about the "super" fort. Visits by ships of Her Majesty's Navy were not always friendly. More than once the gunboats called at Fort Rupert to keep the peace with blue-jackets and cannons.

the few Europeans under him, had been under considerable apprehension for the safety of the fort."

Adding to poor Weynton's problems had been the fact that several of his own men had joined in the "debauch!"

"The natives, on my landing," Richards continued, "were gathered in a state of great excitement on account, as they alleged, of the late murder of one of their chiefs, T-coosma, by the Songhie (Songhees) tribe at Victoria. They were evidently at the same time much alarmed at the visit of the two ships and anxious that I should give them assurance that we had come with no hostile intentions towards them.

"I told the chiefs that I would talk to them on the following morning, and I recommended them to return to their lodges, which they shortly did. On consulting with Mr. Weynton, the very intelligent and circumspect officer commanding. . .and learning from him the feelings of the natives generally as also his suspicion that they intended to organize a large force by collecting the neighboring tribes, to go to the southward and avenge the murder of the Chief T-coosma. . .I decided to take advantage of the presence of the two ships, and lecture the chiefs on the impropriety of their conduct. I accordingly landed on the morning of the 14th, accompanied by Commander Pearse and some of the officers and requested the chiefs to meet me in the fort."

The chieftains declined to enter the fort enclosure and Captain Richards compromised by meeting them outside the palisades. There, with the assistance of an interpreter provided by Weynton, he "explained to them that the governor was very angry with them, as well as with the other tribes generally, in consequence of the frequent murders that had lately been committed as well as their practice of carrying each other off into slavery. I told them that the time had come when these things must cease, that they all, like ourselves, were subjects of the Queen, and were amenable to her laws, and that if they had any grievance to complain of, the proper course was for one of their chiefs to go to the governor; if any of their people were murdered or taken into slavery, they were not to murder innocent men in retaliation, but that the real offender, if he could be captured, would be tried by our laws and if found guilty, hanged.

"They replied that it was an Indian custom to kill all they could if one of their people was killed; that they were not worse than the other tribes; that what I said was 'good,' and if the others would leave off murdering they would.

"At this stage of the proceedings the brother of the murdered man, T-coosma, stood up and declared his intention of collecting all the people who were friendly to the Rupert Indians to go down and kill every Indian they could meet with southwards of Nanaimo. He, and many of the others, was in a most excited state and it was some time before I could prevail on him to listen to me.

"He at last became, in measure, pacified by my assuring him that if his brother had been murdered in Victoria, and the murderer could be apprehended, the governor would assuredly cause him to be hanged; and I would strongly urge if some such example were made at Victoria it would have a most beneficial effect on all the neighboring tribes."

Thanks to the arrival of HM ships *Plumper* and *Alert*, "another of the terrifying forays that had decimated the southern tribes" was averted.

This was not always the case. More than once, the arrival of British warships at Fort Rupert meant death and destruction for the natives who had settled there, when sailors burned down their long houses in retaliation for their refusal to surrender those tribesmen allegedly guilty of murder. Most famous of these unhappy incidents is that of the tragedy which led to the christening of the nearby Deserter Islands. . . .

Almost from the beginning the HBC had had problems with its miners — Vancouver Island's first immigrants. To work its new coal deposits the company had imported professionals from the Old Country. Among them was a young man whose name would become synonymous with coal the length of the Pacific Coast: Robert Dunsmuir. Hired as foreman at the age of 26, the ambitious Scotsman landed on the lonely shores of northern Vancouver Island in 1851 with his wife Joan, two daughters and infant son, James, who had been born during the voyage to the New World. Ironically in light of his later achievements, Dunsmuir's initial assignment at Fort Rupert was inauspicious as the fledging mine was soon rated to be a failure.

Not all of Fort Rupert's miners were as determined to succeed as was Dunsmuir. As far as the HBC was concerned, few wanted to work at all. At first they rebelled against the working conditions, isolation and their food, demanding beer, spirits and wine as part of their daily rations. These, the HBC contended, were mere red herrings, as news of the California gold rush had reached them. Now all that the miners wanted to do was to break their contracts with the HBC. As a result, several of the more obdurate were put in irons and placed on bread and water.

The diaries of one of these miners, Andrew Muir, show that the difficulties at Rupert were two-sided. His chief complaint was to the effect that the Scottish miners — intensely proud of the fact that they were professionals — had been asked to do work as common labourers. This was beneath their dignity and in violation of their contracts. "Now we are in Vancouver (Island) and we are put to the sinking of a pit to look for coal, a thing we never agreed to, and to do all manner of work, and I consider the Company has broken our agreement, as we were only to work as laborers in the event of the coal not succeeding."

Of great irritation, he wrote, was the HBC's unwillingness to construct a protective palisade about the pithead or to provide armed escorts for its miners. Muir and his comrades had no illusions as to the neighbouring Nahwitties' friendliness as, time and again, they had seen warriors venture forth and "in five minutes return with two of their neighbors heads in their hands."

Relations between the miners and HBC officials became even more strained when the former were ordered to dig a well and drains within the fort. This, the miners refused to do unless the HBC directive was put in writing and it was acknowledged that, if they were to be labourers, they were not to be miners. But, penned Muir, George Blenkinsop, clerk in charge of the fort during Captain McNeil's absence, refused to do this and threatened them all with the direst penalties while waving a sword and pistol. After accusing Muir and fellow workman John McGregor of instigating a sit-down strike, Blenkinsop ordered both placed in irons for six days.

This unhappy state of affairs came to a tragic head for brothers George and Charles Wishart, and Fred Watkins. Having deserted their own ship in Victoria the three seamen stowed away aboard the HBC bark *England* for a free ride to the goldfields. When the *England* reached Fort Rupert, where it was to load coal for California, several of the disgruntled miners agreed to join them. Then, to everyone's dismay, the *Beaver* anchored in the harbour.

Jumping to the conclusion that she was after them, Wishart and Watkins fled into the woods. When the *Beaver* went on her way, Dr. J.S. Helmcken, HBC physician who also acted as magistrate, sent word to the seamen that it was unsafe for them to remain at large in hostile Indian country, that they should return at once to the fort.

The deserters disregarded Helmcken's warning. Several days after, near Shushartie, they were discovered by three Nahwittie braves. Upon the natives' approach the whites panicked and, hoping to scare them off, waved an axe, threw rocks and cursed. Later claiming that they had not meant the whites any harm, but that they had been outraged by their belligerence, the warriors chased them into the woods. Within minutes the deserters had been hacked to pieces, their bodies concealed.

Word of the atrocity soon reached the fort, where the miners, who accused the HBC of having instigated the "massacre," became terrified of an all-out Indian assault. For their part the Nahwitties were emboldened by the incident and, when the miners fled the safety of the fort for Shushartie, they made plans to overrun the few officers who had remained at their posts.

The tribesmen became more antagonistic by the hour, some even climbing the palisades to "leer down at the unhappy whites, who," the record explains, "realized that any demonstration (on their part) would be the signal for an attack." Happily for the besieged whites, they were saved from what seemed imminent destruction by the timely arrival of yet another HBC vessel, the *Mary Dare*.

The impetuous miners returned to the fort when Gov. Richard Blanshard arrived on the scene aboard the warship HMS *Daedalus*. Upon learning of the recent crisis, Blanshard and Capt. G.R. Wellesley, commander of the *Daedalus*, agreed that Dr. Helmcken should meet with Chief Nancy of the Nahwitties to negotiate the surrender of the guilty parties. Accompanied only by a French Canadian half-breed named Battineau, Helmcken ventured into the Nahwittie camp. Fortunately for them, Chief Nancy was able to keep his several hundred men, all armed and eager to do battle, in check. During an all-night parley Nancy admitted that members of his tribe were guilty of the murders, but would not agree to their surrender. It was Indian law in such cases, he explained, to make reparations — but no more. When Helmcken insisted that the murderers must be surrendered for trial and, if found guilty, punished by hanging, he refused to discuss the issue further.

Upon Helmcken's reporting this to the governor aboard the *Daedalus*, Blanshard ordered Captain Wellesley to take the

Fort Rupert's famous 18-foot-stockade, from which the warlike Nahwitties leered down at the frightened whites.

Nahwittie village by force. The next morning a force of bluejackets, under command of Lieutenant Burton, stormed the Indian encampment, to find it abandoned. Following his instructions Burton put all long houses and canoes to the torch.

Apparently content with this stern reprisal, and short of supplies, Wellesley set sail for California — but not before a brief skirmish with the hostile natives, who somewhat evened the score by wounding an officer and two seamen.

There matters rested for several months. During the lull, the Nahwitties began construction of a formidable new encampment on an island in Bull Harbour. The following summer HMS *Daphnae* arrived on the scene to, in the words of Blanshard's soon-to-be successor, Chief Factor James Douglas, "carr(y) it by assault, in the midst of a severe fire from the natives. . . ." When a "body of white faces" did storm the Indian stockades, they found that the defenders had fled, leaving only their dead and wounded. Once again white man's justice demanded complete destruction of the village. This time, Douglas noted, "All their property and provisions were captured and destroyed together with about 20 fine canoes — so that they have sustained a very severe loss. The tribe is now completely dispersed and are reported to be some where on the West side of the Island."

When Governor Blanshard posted a reward for the three murderers, who had not been captured in either engagement, the disheartened Nahwitties ordered the men to surrender to justice. Not surprisingly, they refused to do so, with the result that two were slain by their own tribesmen, and the third escaped. To close the case the Nahwitties substituted the body of a slave, carried the "mangled remains" to Fort Rupert — and demanded the reward. There, after the bodies were duly identified by "the chiefs of the Quakiolth tribes," they were buried near the post and the case finally closed.

The mishandling of this affair led to Governor Blanshard's submitting his resignation — a curious conclusion to one of British Columbia's earliest and most exciting murder cases.

Ships of Her Majesty's Navy found it necessary to call at Fort Rupert from time to time to keep the peace (although some question exists as to the legitimacy of all such punitive expeditions). In 1866 HMS *Clio*, Captain Turnour commanding, bombarded the village causing several casualties.

But Fort Rupert's days of infamy were ending. With the closing of the mines the fort assumed a new aura of respectability as a trading post — with but the odd relapse to earlier ways. In the spring of 1872 a *Colonist* correspondent, "writing from near Fort Rupert," reported that "feasts on human flesh are very common among the Indians in that neighborhood. One tribe will sacrifice a slave or a child and peddle the meat from camp to camp. The horrid feast commences at the full of the December moon, and during its progress the partakers appear to be more like wild beasts than human beings. We had thought and hoped that cannibalism had died out among the native tribes of British Columbia."

However, if civilization was gaining at the historic outpost, the trading of furs and salmon (smoked and exported to the Sandwich Islands) was steadily falling off. In 1873 the HBC sold out to its factor, Robert Hunt, a Dorsetshire man who had joined its ranks as a labourer in 1850. Hunt continued to use the decaying fort as living quarters. Finally, in the spring of 1889, Fort Rupert was no more. A *Colonist* headline declared: FIRE AT FORT RUPERT; AN OLD LANDMARK REMOVED BY THE FLAMES.

Actually, something of the old stockade and remaining buildings survived this latest threat by holocaust, only the 90-foot by 40-foot officers' quarters being consumed. Twenty-six years before, an Indian woman, locked in her home by a jealous lover, accidentally started a fire when she left a small lamp burning too close to her bedside. The poor girl died in the ensuing blaze, which also destroyed four houses in the village and threatened the fort before being brought under control by officers of the HBC and Captain Lewis and his men of the visiting HBC steamer *Labouchere*.

Over the years, what little remained became salvage: two-inch-thick floorboards which had been tongue-and-grooved by hand, and 16-inch-thick rafters and window sills were cut up and burned as firewood.

Today little remains of either Fort Rupert or the village of Ku-Kultz beyond the former's chimney, constructed of local stone and lime mortar manufactured from clamshells, the old Cadwallader store and the iron-railed Robert Hunt family plot.

For some reason Fort Rupert's commemorative plaque has had to be situated farther down the road. Another intriguing memento of a forgotten past is Beaver Harbour's bank of clamshells. For centuries before the building of Fort Rupert and Ku-Kultz, Indians had taken advantage of the safe harbour here and the plentiful clams. As evidence of the latter, a bed of discarded shells — with an occasional chunk of lignite from the old mines — was an incredible two miles long, one-half mile wide, and 50 feet deep. Much of the nearby Port Hardy airport was surfaced with shells from this midden.

Perhaps the most fascinating link with old Fort Rupert is the ancient Hunt store, built after the fire and owned by his descendants, the Cadwallader family. Crumbling and closed, it recalls a fabulous era. The Cadwallader family has in their possession several of the old store ledgers which contain many tantalizing entries, such as that of November 21, 1890, when it is noted that $96.50 had been stolen from the till. Storekeeper Cadwallader, who was up to such emergencies, records how he tracked two Indian suspects, accused them of the theft, and demanded restitution. The next day, a short entry concludes the incident: "The money was returned, and that settles the matter." ♣

Cape Scott

I F ever there was a land of broken dreams, that land was Vancouver Island's northwestern tip — Cape Scott.

It was here, at the close of the 19th century, that a number of settlers chose to battle the elements and the isolation to build a colony in the wilderness. That they failed seems, today, to have been inevitable. Yet, there is something noble about their joust with fate and, more than three-quarters of a century after, one cannot help but admire those hardy pioneers who were willing to challenge the unknown with nothing more than raw courage, a strong back and a sharp axe.

But the history of the area goes back much further. In 1786, James Strange, trading for the East Indian Company, left Bombay with two vessels, the *Captain Cook* and *Experiment,* in search of sea otter skins. The 300-ton *Captain Cook* was under the command of Captain Lowrie, while the smaller *Experiment* was under the command of Captain Guise. On August 1 Strange sighted a chain of seven islands, which he named the Scott Islands and claimed for King George III. Recording the event in his journal, Strange wrote: "This being our first discovery during the expedition, it naturally followed that I should give them a name whereby they may hereafter be known. I accordingly named them after the Patron of this Expedition, my most respected friend, Mr. David Scott." Continuing to the northern tip of Vancouver Island, Strange rounded the cape, which came to be known as Cape Scott, and made his way down the eastern coastline.

Eventually, the fur trade exhausted the supply of sea otter pelts on the coast, and with it declined much of Britain's interest. Thus, it was for an entirely different reason that a new group was lured to the Cape 110 years later. Interest in the area was stimulated quite by accident when a Danish immigrant visited the area in 1894. Rasmus Hansen, aboard the Seattle fishing schooner *Floyberg,* had gone ashore in Goose Harbour hunting for ducks. Exploring the lagoon that lay at its head, Hansen discovered a large stretch of tidal meadows, through which ran two streams, both filled with salmon. It was then that he conceived the idea of establishing a Danish settlement on the site, similar to the Norweigan settlements at Quatsino and Bella Coola.

Hansen convinced three other prospective colonists, Y.

(Opposite page) A section of the Cape Scott trail, featuring boardwalk. (Left inset) Bernt Ronning's Cape Scott homestead, with monkey trees, c1983. (Right inset) The wheel and hub of a once sturdy buckboard.
(Below) The sand neck, Cape Scott, c1910. Pioneer settler N.P. Jensen grew clover on land reclaimed from sand dune. (Inset) Hauling hay in home-made solid-wheel wagon on the sand neck.

Chris Jensen, Peter Thomasen and Nels C. Nelson, of the location's potential and, after a visit to the site in 1896, the four wrote a letter to the British Columbia government outlining their colonization project. The Hon. James Baker replied that the government was prepared to open the land for colonization, free of charge, and promised to build roads. Encouraged by this response, Hansen and Nelson landed at Fisherman's Bay in the fall of 1896 and quickly erected a house from driftwood. After building a skiff, Hansen returned to Seattle to encourage settlers while Nelson wintered at the colony site.

A series of articles in Danish-language newspapers published in Cedar Falls, Iowa, and Omaha, Nebraska, coupled with meetings held in cities and towns along the west coast, attracted a small number of daring souls willing to venture into the unknown wilderness. According to *The Cape Scott Story,* the articles had painted a picture of an idyllic settlement. "Ninety acres of land, 10 of natural meadow and 80 of bush or timber, could be had for nothing more than some work on improving it. Waters teemed with fish, ducks, and geese; and the land was plentifully supplied with deer. Above all, the colonist could find independence; freedom from the punch-card of mine and mill; opportunity to set his stamp on a new society in a new untouched land."

In March, 1897, the first expedition of colonists sailed north on the *Floyberg,* which had been purchased for the co-operative by Hansen. After transporting settlers to the site, the *Floyberg* was to be used as a supply ship and for halibut fishing. While she sailed in the ocean along Vancouver Island's west coast, the main body of colonists travelled up the sheltered waters of the inside passage between Vancouver Island and the B.C. mainland in the chartered *Willipa.*

The fate of these two vessels should have given the colonists an indication of what life at the northern tip of Vancouver Island would be like. In stormy weather, the *Floyberg's* main boom broke off Cape Cook. Despite this, the men were able to sail the crippled vessel into Fisherman's Bay. But their troubles were not over. During the night a sudden swell forced them to cut anchor and make sail. They fought their way around the Cape again, to Goose Harbour. There, with no anchor, the crew was forced to beach the schooner. It broke adrift, however, and was damaged beyond repair. The *Willipa* was also wrecked just after her trip to Fisherman's Bay, but was purchased by Capt. John Irving and put back into service.

It was the Cape's vulnerability to storm that prompted the first settlers to choose the somewhat more sheltered Fisherman's Bay as their landing site and base camp for those to follow. Subsequently the provincial government, which had done everything possible to encourage the Danish colonists, dispatched a surveyor to subdivide the grassy meadows of the lagoon and to designate a number of sections.

Somewhat to the homesteaders' surprise, they found that they did not have the area, as isolated as it was, to themselves. Cape Scott was playing host to scores of prospectors who zealously panned and picked their way along every streambed and beach in their search for valuable minerals. However, with the worldwide excitement of the Klondike, most of the miners were off to the north, and the settlers were left alone with their dreams.

First item on the agenda was a road — or at least a reasonable facsimile. As their nearest "neighbour" seemed to be the outpost of Shushartie, on the east coast of the island, the dauntless Danes, after constructing homes of split-cedar planks and shakes, squared their shoulders and hacked a trail

overland. The first few miles, from the lagoon to Fisherman's Bay, was developed into a passable corduroyed wagon road as the initial homesteads by the shore began to be joined by others. Soon the little "colony" was expanding to landward.

As more settlers arrived, the area assumed an almost civilized appearance. Where, but months before, had been virgin meadow and forest, homes, outbuildings, fences and the first vegetable crops made their debut. Most pioneers were able to live off the land as far as meat, fowl and fish were concerned, as the cape area abounded in wild fowl, deer and bear. Offshore, salmon and halibut formed another ready source of food, as, ever so painfully, the Danes began to beat back the forest.

In 1898, according to *The Cape Scott Story,* "C.W. Rasmussen and Theo Fredericksen dragged their dismantled sawmill some three miles to the Fisherman River with a team of horses, then floated it, piece by piece, down the stream, to reassemble it at a site convenient for their purpose. A dory, a parsonage, timbers for dike sluice gates, and the colony's first freight and passenger vessel, the *Cape Scott,* were some of the varied uses to which lumber from this mill was put during the few years it operated."

Meanwhile, Cape Scott's "business" centre was N.C. Nelson's store, operated on a cooperative basis, at Fisherman's Bay. Soon the growing settlement had a community hall, which doubled as a school, a post office, in Nelson's store, a Danish language newspaper (the *Sandfly*) and a population of 90 souls.

But, already, some difficulties had arisen which, despite every effort, had not been surmounted. Perhaps the greatest disappointment and, ultimately, one of the greatest physical blows to the settlers' master plan, was their failure to start a commercial halibut fishery. Those who had expected to earn a steady living by this means had no choice but to venture to Rivers Inlet, 60 miles distant by open sea, during the annual sockeye run.

Another devastating blow came in the form of a gale which smashed their dyking system in the lagoon. Here, an ambitious program had been undertaken to reclaim the tidal flats by use of dykes of driftwood, the new and fertile area thus formed being subdivided into 10-acre lots. But the elements had other plans. On the very night of the celebration to mark their completion, the dykes were demolished.

Despite the hardships and setbacks the pioneers held on, their determination attracting even more colonists, as well as the provincial government's concern. Finally, in 1899, the government informed the colony that no further leases would be let at Cape Scott. Lester Peterson, author of *The Cape Scott Story,* who was born at San Josef Bay, wrote: "The colonist knew that the decision had originated in a belief that if large numbers of some one ethnic group were given exclusive rights to settle some particular area, regardless of how remote or how restricted the size of this area, this group would possibly not assimilate rapidly enough into some undefined Canadian way of life.

"It is rather interesting to note that, while British Columbia was doubting the sincerity, and perhaps fearing the strength, of fewer than 100 immigrants of Danish ancestry to assimilate, many hundreds of Doukhobors were being invited into the province under quite special considerations.

"While the Cape Scott settlers were required to put up bonds of $50 per family, to pay their transportation to the colony, and while they were expected to build their own homes, church, school, and dike, the new immigrants into the Kootenays were transported free of charge to commodious brick homes provided for them at general revenue expense."

The government then reneged on its promise to construct a road to Quatsino Sound, as called for in the fourth year of the colony. This natural isolation proved to be another crippling blow to the young colony as most settlers had counted upon growing produce for market. Because they were totally cut off from the rest of Vancouver Island they soon had to face the fact that they could not sell their crops "outside"; and they certainly could not sell to each other. This meant that it was useless to grow more than each family could consume at its own table. And another dream died.

As the original settlers began to realize the hopelessness of their efforts and leave the settlement, others, encouraged by newspaper accounts of the idyllic conditions, arrived to try their luck. Most of these later arrivals chose to establish in the San Josef Valley, while others preferred Holberg (due east of San Josef Bay), Sea Otter Cove (just north of the bay), or Shushartie, where a small settlement was born. Soon these newcomers also appreciated the utter loneliness of their chosen homes. Linked to each other only by a spider web of trails through dense forest, their outlet to the sea blocked through most of the year by storms, often with winds up to 80 miles an hours, and beset by rains which continued throughout most of winter and summer, they became disillusioned. (Snow, it might be mentioned, was not a problem because of the passing Japanese Current; this mildness contributed to the successful crops grown here.) Game became scarce because of the increased hunting and trapping, and their livestock either wandered off into the bush or fell victim to cougars.

When it finally became apparent that the noble experiment was not working, the government interceded with the suggestion that the outlying families move to the more densely populated San Josef Valley. If they agreed to this move the province would build a road between San Josef Bay and Holberg. By this time most of the settlers had had enough of government promises — and enough of the hardships of Cape Scott. Rather than move to the San Josef Valley and abandon everything they had worked for, most opted to leave altogether. As more and more new settlers arrived at San Josef and Holberg, the original Cape Scott pioneers moved out, some to either of the nearby settlements, others to begin life anew in "civilization."

Soon only two, Nels Jensen and Theo Frederickson, remained. Then, in 1909, the tragedy was re-enacted. New settlers started to arrive — on a government assurance that a road would be built. This time the boom was in earnest. As more and more families poured into the region, plans for colonization became more elaborate — at least, bigger if not better.

This time the government stood by its promise. Not only was a road to Holberg begun, but a telegraph line was completed between Holberg, Cape Scott and Shushartie, with links between San Josef Bay and Sea Otter Cove.

Most of the recent arrivals settled in San Josef Valley, and by 1913 every available pre-emption had been taken. Holberg, rather than being overshadowed by its western neighbour, became the commercial axis for the entire tip of the Island, most traffic having to pass through Holberg regardless of destination. As work on the wagon road to San Josef progressed, traffic naturally increased and it has been estimated that, by 1914, the region's population had grown to 1,000 persons as tiny homesteads were hacked from a protesting forest from Holberg to San Josef to Cape Scott.

Most had been attracted to the area by reports of its rich soil and temperate climate. For those who originally pre-empted in these locations, it was true enough. But the arable land was extremely limited and, for most latecomers, just not available. Rather than return to their original homes, or locate elsewhere, these colonists, most of whom were new to the dubious joys of homesteading, insisted on attempting to turn wilderness into farmland. As was to be expected, few succeeded.

For that matter few remained long enough to find out. When 1914 brought world war and a call to arms, most of the patriotic young bachelors marched away to enlist, and work on the essential road stopped as abruptly.

Once again the homesteads were surrendered to the rain forests as more and more joined the exodus. With peacetime, four years later, some returned, only to realize the futility of it all and move away forever. By 1930 only a handful remained throughout the entire region. Then the wilderness was undisputed monarch once more. In the late 1930s logging operations were begun in the area of Holberg, which became an air force base during the Second World War.

By this time the only inhabitants of Cape Scott were those airmen stationed at a radar station built there in answer to the threat of Japanese invasion. All of the others had gone. Where men and women had struggled to create homesteads, only a few crumbling ruins remained to tell of their labours. Their fields, marked by fallen fences, were overgrown, and human visitors were reduced to timber cruisers and the occasional prospector who marvelled at the startling sight of wild cattle and stunted fruit trees in the middle of nowhere.

For those modern-day adventurers willing to make the hike into Cape Scott, many of these haunting memorials to a tragic past remain — not to mention the area's incredibly rugged beauty, its golden sands and its wild-wizened trees. Ruins of many of the old homesteads are to be found throughout the region; most are overgrown by brush and blackberry canes. Some of the rotting homes are partially furnished. Up until recent years it was not uncommon to enter a long-abandoned house and see it almost as its owner had left it; pictures on the walls, books and correspondence on a desk, wood neatly piled beside the stove, plates and utensils on the table. Most revealing signs of the original inhabitant's lengthy absence were the spider webs and mice. In a barn, harness still hung from a nail. In an overgrown field: the ghost of a hay wagon, with its handmade wooden wheels "just waiting for the team to be hitched up." Not everything was left to the forest, however. One former resident recalled a neighbouring family who had carried away everything they could manage in their arms and on their backs, including a box containing three cats.

If only these ruins could speak! Some, in fact, in their own way, do tell a story. The bones of the old community hall-schoolhouse are flattened now but, underneath the rubble, the school desks hide. Once, all-night dances had attracted settlers from miles around. Eager participants, who had been informed of forthcoming festivities by notices nailed to trees, walked from as far away as Holberg and San Josef Bay. Some structures of the wartime radar station of the Cape yet stand, although all were looted, immediately upon being abandoned, of their bathroom fixtures. Apparently some of the happy owners found the 20th-century convenience too heavy as, occasionally, one can find them discarded beside the long trail to Holberg.

(Above) The grave of William Christensen who died tragically of blood poisoning on October 17, 1903.

(Right) The Jim Cordy homestead in 1982. This was formally the home of Knute Hansen.

(Below) The west coast of Vancouver Island at Cape Scott.

(Above) Early Danish-speaking Cape Scott colonists. C.W. Rasmussen (coveralls) seated in front of stump, left, beside N.C. Nelson (shirt). Soren Simonsen (cap) leaning on stump behind Nelson.
(Below) The remains of the army plank road at Guise Bay, 1983.

(Above) The Cape Scott light station. Notice the manicured lawns and gardens, characteristic of B.C.'s light stations.
(Below) A grave on the sand neck, Cape Scott, in 1982.
(Bottom) A plough found at Spencer's farm in 1982.

Cape Scott 73

*(Above) Capt. Henry Petersen and Mrs.
Petersen at Sea Otter Cove in 1915.
(Right) The unfinished little Cape Scott
church at the time of its only wedding in
1916. Situated on the San Josef River a
short distance from San Josef Bay, it collapsed about 1914.*

At Shushartie, blackberry canes run rampant among the few old buildings. Few visitors are aware that this little community once boasted a cannery and hotel, about as civilized as any of the Cape Scott communities ever became.

Other monuments to man's struggle in the wilderness are more noticeable. Nels Jensen, who died in 1934, lies buried at Guise Bay, his grave and headstone surrounded by a white picket fence. Another lonely headstone at Cape Scott is that of schoolteacher Chris Christensen's young son. Eight feet tall, and of pink granite, it bears the inscription: "William, Adopted son of C.B. Christensen, died Oct. 17, 1906. Aged 12 years, 9 mo's. The sun went down while it was yet day."

The tragic death of young Christensen emphasised the community's isolation. The boy, walking barefoot, stepped on a rusty nail. Blood poisoning set into an otherwise trivial wound, but because the nearest hospital, at Alert Bay, was 70 miles by rough sea, no small boat could make the trip. Fortunately, the death of Christensen was the only one attributed to the isolation.

In 1969 another old time resident, Mrs. Caroline Moen, recalled what it had been like to live at Cape Scott. She was eight when her parents moved there "about 1898." The family homesteaded on 160 acres and lived in a cabin built of driftwood planks during construction of a two-room log cabin. But the family experienced tragedy when both her sister and brother died. Her mother, she recalled, was the third woman to arrive at Cape Scott and, for a time, supplemented the family income by selling fresh butter to the ships which called from Victoria. Although the settlers experienced shortages of meat and flour when the steamers were delayed by storm, she said they seldom lacked fresh fruit, oats or potatoes, and

there were always shellfish at the beach.

"As a child I remember that beautiful, sandy beach. We called it Sunset Beach. We often played on the logs and picnicked and picked big, fat wild strawberries which grew down among the logs." But, within a year and a half, her parents, having lost two children and weary of the continuing struggle to get by, packed up their possessions, like so many others who were to follow.

In the fall of 1969, the provincial government announced that it had swapped rights to $10 million worth of timber for title to 576 acres at Cape Scott. The new park reserve included the historic Danish settlement. Although the government came under heavy fire for its lopsided bargain — the park-land was estimated to be worth only $300,000, as apposed to the value of the timber stands — most conservationists and recreationists welcomed this latest addition to the provincial parks stable. Completely unspoiled by development, and still unconnected to the outside world by road, it is a wonderland to a steadily increasing number of visitors. Due to its isolation, much of the region is unchanged from the day the original settlers gathered up what few possessions they could carry and walked away. Vandalism, happily, has not yet made much of an appearance here, the damage to be seen having been caused by the elements and the years.

The heroic story of Cape Scott lives on. All who come here marvel at the courage of the settlers of old. Those familiar with the story of Cape Scott can truly appreciate one disheartened pioneer's observation of three-quarters of a century ago: "We are on the right island, but on the wrong end and 50 years to soon."

And indeed they were!   ♣

Zeballos

"Rotten Row" — Main Street, Zeballos, 1938. For years the mining town on the west coast of Vancouver Island was accessible only by ship and aircraft. Nevertheless, in a matter of months the town had "fine hotels, well-stocked stores, a bank, school, progressive newspaper, (and) library." Years after the streets were graded with wastes from the mines, someone had a brain wave that the early sorting methods had not been efficient — that the town streets were "paved with gold." A miniature gold rush resulted when residents proceeded to "high-grade" the roadways for their remaining ores.

ALTHOUGH the actual townsite of Zeballos did not appear on the map until the late 1930s, the history of the little mining town goes back much farther — as much as 200 years. For it was in the late 1700s that the Spanish first began to explore this lonely region, not in quest of sea otter pelts, which attracted most American and British traders during this period, but in search for gold. Capt. Alexandro Malespina and his lieutenants Joseph de Espinosa and Ciriaco de Cevallos (after whom the town of Zeballos would later be named), were convinced that, somewhere along the jagged shores of the Pacific Northwest, they would find mines as rich as those of Central and South America. There, Spain had conquered a previously unknown world and become one of the richest nations on earth through the systematic pillaging of a continent.

Surely, they reasoned, there was more gold to be found for the royal coffers, and they began to look northward along the Pacific Coast. Incredibly, the Spaniards did find gold, and lots of it. In the Spanish archives there is reference to a single shipment of gold from the west coast of Vancouver Island. Its value, three-quarters of a million dollars!

"The Spaniards' gold," noted Bruce McKelvie, "was mostly

— if not all — from placer workings. There are evidences, however, that they did some lode mining. They certainly believed that there was 'gold in them thar hills,' and they dreamed of the day when the mountain masses would be mined and yellow ingots would be shipped from the West Coast."

Then the Spanish were gone, forced to cede all interests in the Northwest to the British by treaty after an international incident which almost led to war. With them went the secret of their gold mines, and the source of their fortune became a matter of local legend. Many pondered the mystery, but few were willing to leave the comfort and safety of their armchairs for a first-hand look until early this century, when a handful of prospectors began to probe the maze of mountains and fjords which form Vancouver Island's west coast.

Shortly before the First World War several unidentified "old timers found some very rich gold specimens around the Cape Cook area. . .(and) placer gold was recovered from a creek somewhere between Cape Cook and Kyuquot Sound."

As for the future township of Zeballos, serious interest in this region's gold mining potential did not result in much beyond prospecting until 1924 (one of the earliest to search

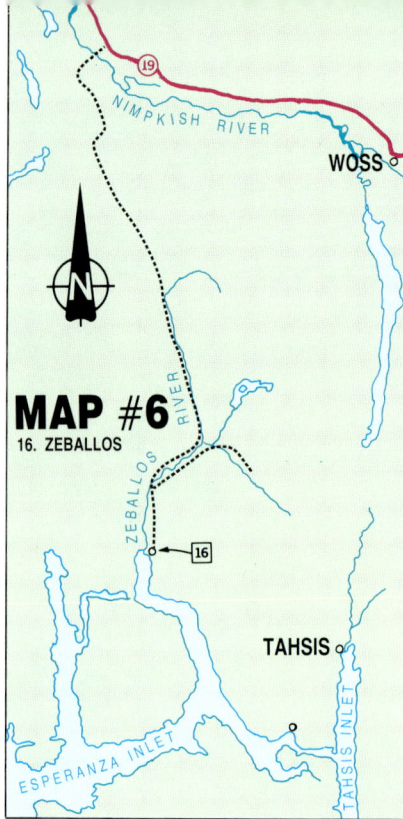

MAP #6

16. ZEBALLOS

WOSS

NIMPKISH RIVER

ZEBALLOS RIVER

16

TAHSIS

ESPERANZA INLET

TAHSIS INLET

(Above) A fishing boat unloading salmon at the Zeballos fish-packing plant.

(Opposite page) During the flood of March, 1940, the main street of Zeballos (Rotten Row) was covered by five feet of water and 20 trees were damaged. (Top inset) This cabin, built by Andy Morod, was the first building in Zeballos. Morod committed suicide by shooting himself in 1983. Apparently he became very depressed when his ability to return to his mountain cabin was prevented by crutches. (Bottom inset) The Zeballos Hotel, originally built in 1936 as the Pioneer Hotel, was purchased by Joe Fisher in 1983. It still serves as a "gathering place" for everyone in town.

(Below) When this photo was taken in 1986, Zeballos was a town of about 250. It had one hotel, two motels (one with one unit, the other with three) and a small general store.

here having been T.J. Marks, in 1907), when a group of claims known as the Tagore group (originally the Eldorado) was staked within a mile and a half of tidewater, on the Zeballos River. Five years and several owners later, the threat of flooding halted development and interest focused upon the King Midas property instead. Activity in the area remained sporadic, despite the fact that, in 1929, the Tagore had made the first shipment, two tons of high-grade ore, from the valley. That same year about 40 claims were staked.

In 1936 Victoria lawyer David S. Tait formed a syndicate with Ray Pitre, Herb Kevis, Chester Canning, Joe and Lou Pednealt, and John Frumento. Incorporated as the Nootka-Zeballos Gold Mines Limited, the new company later changed to Privateer Mine Limited.

That December Pitre, Kevis, Canning and Frumento went to work on the property, four miles from the beach, and drove a tunnel deep into the hillside above the canyon of Spud Creek. It was the depth of winter and, "housed under canvas," they battled cold, rain and mud. Short of funds, they had to improvise as best they could and constructed an aerial tramline of salvaged materials. It was makeshift, but it worked. Supplies and equipment had to be packed in along a steep and slippery trail, the weary miners often becoming bogged down in the mire. Only their faith in their property kept them going as, in the city, David Tait worked just as hard to find the money so necessary to further development. When, despite his every effort, he was unable to secure outside financing, Tait and his law partner, Percy Marchant, took the plunge, pledged their own credit, and borrowed $25,000.

At the mine winter had slowed development to a crawl, and it was not until March, 1938, that the partners made their first shipment of ore. Although a "mere" 4,800 pounds, it represented a massive achievement in itself, as it had had to be taken to the beach, nearly five miles distant, "through a rugged, almost impassable country. Pitre and his little crew," McKelvie continued, "determined to get it out, for the smelter returns were necessary to keep operations going. It was a terrible task. Those who took part in that work still shudder at the remembrance of it. The ore was sacked and was carried on the backs of men down the narrow, slippery trail, through the mud and over the windfalls to Zeballos River. There, a flat bottom boat was built, and in this way they went down the stream to land near the mouth of the river and again back-pack the ore to the beach. That small shipment of 4,800 pounds yielded $2,605 or roughly 54 cents a pound."

Thus inspired (if not exhausted), the partners returned to work with renewed energy and, by the end of 1937, had earned more than $116,000 for the shipments of ore made to the Tacoma smelter. In the first nine months of 1938 almost $200,000 was recovered, and a large eastern mining firm agreed to build a 75-ton cyanide mill and powerhouse and to provide technical advice to the flourishing company. By this time five levels had been developed on the property and it was reported that "such is the richness, and the persistency of the veins, that although only about 2,400 feet of underground workings have been effected so far, reserves sufficient to run the mill for three years, and roughly estimated to have a value of $3 million, have been blocked out."

As was to be expected, others began to take notice when assay reports of the "wonder mine" — 30 to 45 ounces of gold to the ton — became known. "Some of the ore was so rich," said one mining man, "they shipped it to the smelter in carbide bins, and Tacoma said it was the richest ore and most exten-

sively impregnated with free gold that they had ever received."

Further interest was generated when the Privateer held a public ceremony, at which 120 persons attended, to mark the pouring of the first gold bricks at its new mill.

At the Spud Valley Mine (formerly the Goldfield), work was hindered by an exceptionally heavy snowfall during the winter of 1937-38, although "leading mine operator" A.B. Trites reported that the outlook was better than ever, the operation progressing satisfactorily. Plans for a sawmill, powerhouse, 50-ton gold mill with flotation and cyanide setup, he said, were under way. The mine was so rich, Trites claimed, that the operating policy had been to "pick out the waste and send the rest to the ore dump, rather than the reverse."

At the Golden Gate property, situated less than two miles from tidewater at the head of Zeballos Arm, a contract had been let for the driving of a tunnel at its No. 2 mine, a crew working by hand in two shifts to achieve up to four feet daily. To date the average width of the gold seam was six inches, and yielded between $6 and $232 to the ton. Once a new truck road was completed the Golden Gate found itself to be "admirably located," and its camp accommodations were said to be comfortable.

Other properties, such as the North Star group, Rey Oro, White Star, Zeballos Gold Peak, and Central Zeballos, offered equally optimistic reports. At the Privateer, miners encountered a "slab" of high-grade ore that was a foot wide and assayed at 30 ounces to the ton. In just a year the Privateer had put Zeballos on the map and latecomers mourned the fact that, but months before, they could have purchased a share in the property for less than $10,000.

Not all were as fortunate. A miner named Conrad Wolfe acquired the Tagore property in 1932 and encountered "spectacular ore" in a shallow shaft, assays indicating up to 22 ounces of gold to the ton. However, Wolfe, like his predecessors at this group of claims, was stymied by the ever-present danger of flooding from the Zeballos River and decided to seek a safe site above high water where he could sink another shaft. He proceeded to make a good start on this second shaft, only to be called away by important business matters in the United States. After filling the shaft to the collar with rocks, both to deter the curious and to hide the obvious value of the claim, Wolfe left for the States — where he was unavoidably detained. By the time he was able to return to Zeballos his title to the Tagore had lapsed, and others had restaked the site.

This new outfit also decided to test the ground across the river, and discovered a second rich quartz vein which they named the Golden Gate and Golden Gate No. 2 claims. Together with the Tagore and Nabob, these properties were subsequently acquired by the Golden Gate Zeballos Mines Limited.

On Fault Creek, farther inland, work proceeded on the Buccaneer group of claims, and the Piccadilly, Knutsen, and King Midas (Pioneer) groups.

At the same time, promising reports were coming in from farther afield, the *Western Canada Mining News* devoting a special edition to the Zeballos boom, and observing that discoveries had been made on the Little Zeballos River, east of Zeballos Arm, and that "good prospecting areas are indicated north west to Kyuquot Sound and south east to the Tahsis Basin. There is no doubt that hundreds of men will be prospecting the West Coast of Vancouver Island next year, from Port Alberni to Quatsino Sound."

The greatest single obstacle in the way of rapid development, the editor observed in 1938, was that of transportation. Accessible only by CPR coast ships to Ceepeecee, whose name is derived from the initials of the California Packing Corporation, which operated a cannery there, and by airplane, Zeballos was locked away from the rest of the world. From Ceepeecee, everything from food to equipment had to be brought in to the head of Zeballos, about 12 miles, by small boat, then back-packed into the rugged hills because a road to the goldfield had not been completed. Ore shipments had to be brought out the same wearying, tortuous way, or by pack horse. "Back packers could carry only 50 pounds a trip over the trail and could only make two trips a day." As if this were not enough to keep a prospector busy, "It is said by those who know that prospectors intending to cover the West Coast should remember to carry their gold pans, that small creeks should be tested carefully and creeks yielding colors should be examined and traced with a view to finding bedrock in the creek and along the valley walls. . . .

"Enough descriptions have already been written and told about Zeballos itself to make most people aware of the conditions they will meet on arrival. Until winter with its heavy rains gives way to sunshine and dry spring weather the visitor whether prospector or town settler will meet with much discomfort. Accommodation for the traveller from here to there, and while there, is at a premium. A much needed wharf is now under construction, one hotel is finished and another building. There is only one street now, but doubtless the near future will see the swift march of civilization, a barber shop, a school, a beer parlor, a theatre, a bank, a poolroom, stores, a church — and they will all be there to greet the newcomer. . . ."

In fact, a prospector faced considerably worse than winter rains and lack of accommodation in Zeballos. If he intended to seek his fortune in the hills behind Zeballos Arm, he faced a nightmare of back-breaking trails and creeks which would crush the spirit of most men. As noted, he had to take everything in on his back and bring it out the same way. If he were injured he faced an agonizing race for help, as grimly illustrated by miners John Hagmo and Inar Aston, when, "high up on the glaciers and snow," Aston fell down a crevice and broke his leg.

Hagmo succeeded in pulling his partner from the crevice with their pack ropes. He then faced the terrifying task of rushing Aston to safety. Twelve miles of "fearful walking and climbing conditions" from Zeballos, he made Aston as comfortable as possible. Upon placing Aston's leg in splints below the knee, Hagmo realized that the break had occurred at the ankle and attempted to bend the leg at the knee to improvise a "peg leg." As this also proved to be impracticable, he constructed a crude packboard, secured Aston to its frame, and began the incredible hike to the beach, 12 "long, weary unbelievable" miles away.

"What Hagmo endured and Aston suffered on that terrible trip, only they know. When we realize the kind of country they traversed and the fact that Aston and his pack-stays weighed over 200 pounds, the feat seems well worth recording in the annals of mining for it is only such high courage and tenacity that make possible the initial discovery of the elusive yellow metal. . . ."

Other hopeful prospectors encountered grief in the hills behind Zeballos.

Not all were sympathetic to the struggles of these modern-day argonauts. Sneered a veteran of earlier mining wars, who signed himself "Old Un": "It makes one laugh to hear of what a tough time some of our lavender pants pioneers are having on the West Coast of Vancouver Island. If it goes on there should be a ready sale for bed sox, night caps and hot water bottles, and perhaps powder puffs.

"Just think of it, most of the Zeballos area is five long miles and not more than 10 from the waterfront where they land out of staterooms from steamers. Shades of the pioneers, who cut trails and packed their grub into Cariboo, Cassiar, Dease Lake and the Yukon.

"Really, we must be getting maudlin and soft, and many of our hardy adventurers had best stay within sight of the Neon lights, learn to play the piano and dance the Gal-umph and Chuckabloom."

In Zeballos itself, the tiny shacktown on the beach began to achieve greater respectability, particularly with the establishment of its own newspaper, the Zeballos *Miner,* in the spring of 1938. Its publisher was Jimmy Cullins, "son of an old time mining scout," and well known in western mining camps as publisher and newspaper correspondent. Jimmy had been one of the first to recognize Zeballos' potential and the *Mining News* urged its readers to support the *Miner* as "Jimmy deserves it."

"The town of Zeballos is remarkable. . . ." wrote Bruce McKelvie. "It is hard to believe that the substantial community, with its fine hotels, its well-stocked stores, its bank, electrically lit buildings, school, progressive newspaper, and its library, board of trade, hospital association and club, has come into existence in little more than a year. . . ."

Perhaps best known of Zeballos' early residents was Maj. George Nicholson, M.C., who later wrote a history of the Island's west coast which has enjoyed numerous printings. In 1938 Nicholson, described as a "thorough frontiersman of the West Coast of V.I.," was the settlement's postmaster, mining recorder, transportation agent and "practically uncrowned mayor of the Golden City in Embryo." Among other achievements, Nicholson had been responsible for linking Zeballos to the outside world by radio telephone.

Up until this time newcomers to Zeballos had had to brave a gauntlet of rowboats and waist-deep mud to make it to the beach. Nicholson had carried many of them through the surf on his shoulders, and it was with considerable anticipation that residents greeted an announcement that a contract for a 750-foot wharf had been let to Nickson and Company.

Another legendary figure of the Zeballos saga was bush pilot Ginger Coote, whose exploits and mercy flights would make a book in themselves.

As the mines gained in importance Zeballos continued to gain in stature and population. By the outbreak of the Second World War it boasted 1,000 inhabitants and its first street, Rotten Row, was no longer known by that sobriquet. In fact, the town streets had undergone quite a transformation. Originally the grades had been surfaced with wastes from the nearby mines. When someone concluded that the early sorting operations were not too thorough, a gold rush in miniature took place as residents dug up and "high-graded" the ore-bearing roadways.

But, as with all mining towns, even Zeballos, the town known for its streets paved with gold, the boom is always followed by the bust. During the war scarcity of skilled labour closed down all of the mines, the Privateer being the last to cease production in 1943. In late 1945 work was resumed. But in-

(Above) This view of Zeballos River, with Zeballos Peak in the background, was taken in August, 1986.
(Below) An exterior view of the original Power House building at the Spud Valley gold mine. This mine has been undergoing tests for the last two years with the hopes of reopening.

(Above) The No. 7 adit of Spud Valley mine in 1986.
(Right) The generator in the only building left standing at the Spud Valley mine from the 1930s.
(Below left) A "jaw-crusher" at the Spud Valley mine.
(Below centre) This rusted wall safe was attached to the interior wall of the concentrator building. It was once used to keep the gold bars as well as valuable papers.
(Below right) This "amalgam barrel" was also located in the concentrator building. All these photos were taken on August 19, 1986.

Entrance to the Privateer mine, 1939. During the Second World War a shortage of labour caused a temporary shutdown. With peacetime, increased operating costs and the price of gold fixed at $35 an ounce brought permanent closure. Millions of dollars were extracted here between the years 1936-48.

creased operating costs and the artificially pegged price of gold at $35 an ounce proved to be a fatal combination and Zeballos began to lose its lustre and its population. When the Privateer shut down for the last time in 1948 it had more than earned the title of "wonder mine," for it had been Zeballos' biggest producer, having yielded nearly one-half of the camp's total production. Twenty-five years ago the little settlement staged something of a comeback when an iron mine was established there. Once again the town knew the heavy tread of the miner's "cork-boot" and a lively time in its bars.

In 1962 a Vancouver newspaperman described Zeballos' second grab for the brass ring. "Construction company offices now fill a couple of buildings, headquarters of the new boom, and behind them lights glow in the night through tents pitched on wooden frames. There's the village clerk's office and the community hall, and across the mud of the churned-up street the Pioneer Hotel stretches wide its porch.

"The boardwalks go up and down and disappear altogether. A cafe sheds a patch of light, though it will close early if there's a big 'liquor' dance in the community hall, as there was to celebrate Valentine's Day. It doesn't close early for the regular bingo sessions on Saturday nights.

"The cafe's Saturday customers fling themselves in gaggles of hard-hats and cork-boots into the protesting booths, and bellow for coffee. Or they come in quiet, almost timid, and alone, and find themselves called up to referee an argument they inevitably get drawn into. Others swoop in flaunting their great beards. . . ."

For oldtime residents, it must have been like turning the clock back to 1938. Then the iron mine was history and Zeballos was quiet once more, its population having dwindled to just over 100 souls. By 1968 a third of the town's 70-odd houses were vacant. As Olaf Norhaug remarked with a sad smile, it was nothing like when he arrived in 1938: "The place

was like an army camp. There were tents all over the place and at least 18 bootleggers from the hotel to the water, a distance of about a quarter mile."

In 1973 the price of gold soared to record heights and exploration work by diamond drill was begun on the site of the historic Privateer mine. According to a spokesman for the New Privateer Mine Limited, if the results were encouraging an open-pit operation would be considered. Others had expressed an interest in the region's long talked-about copper deposits.

Not surprisingly, memories of the golden boom of Zeballos which, between 1938 and 1945, yielded more than $13 million, were rekindled.

Three years before Zeballos had been granted an 11th-hour reprieve in the form of an assurance by the Tahsis Logging Company that it would become the firm's logging headquarters. A second bonus for the community, then reduced to 35 residents, was the long-awaited road to the outside. The road to Nimpkish Lake, where it joined with the main provincial highway between Gold River and Port Hardy, was rough. Provincial forests minister Ray Williston described it as "the rawest piece of road some people with us have been over in all their lives."

In 1985, Zeballos received some more good news. Toronto-based McAdam Resources Inc. had restaked the 50-year old Goldfield claim, hoping the Spud Valley property "would become the core asset around which the company will grow." The property was first located in June, 1935, by Sam Knutsen, one of the original prospectors in the Zeballos camp. In July, 1936, A.B. Trites acquired the property from Mr. Knutsen, drove the upper three levels, and built a small camp about 300 feet north of and at about the same elevation as the present No. 6 level. In 1937 Spud Valley Gold Mines Ltd. acquired the property from the Trites' interests, continued underground work on the Goldfield vein, and commenced work on the Spur and Roper veins. The company built a 60-man camp and, late in 1938, a 10-ton-per-day mill. March 1939 production was $38,300, with operating expenses of less than $15,000. The mine was closed in 1942 and a watchman was retained on the property.

Production and operating data for the entire life of the mine shows a total of 186,698 short tons of ore mined. Of this, 105,687 tons were treated to yield 54,039 ounces of gold and 18,475 ounces of silver. Average cost per ton milled at 1940 levels was $10.

McAdam has been conducting a substantial exploration program on the property. The work to date has included re-tracking the No. 7 level and slashing this level to straighten it out; followed by approximately 9,000 feet of underground drilling and 2,000 to 3,000 feet of surface drilling. If the tests and exploration work prove encouraging, a full-blown gold mine would be the results.

Lumbering, fishing and two small gold mines have stabilized the Zeballos population (which, during its most prosperous gold mining years reached 1,500, and during its bleakest period dipped to 35), at about 350. Today's Zeballos has a liquor store, general store, community hall, school and small motel. The 10-room Zeballos Hotel was originally the Pioneer Hotel. Built in 1939 by Les Brown, it was the first hotel built in the valley. Reaching Zeballos is no longer a problem either, its gravel logging-road, although dusty, is well-maintained. Thus, after 50 long, hectic and trying years, Zeballos, the town that wouldn't die, is part of the world at large. ♣

Clayoquot

The boats of HMS Sutlej *and* Devastation *attacking an Indian village in Clayoquot Sound.*

ONCE the unofficial "capital city" of the Island's west coast, from Alberni to Quatsino, Clayoquot has a rich and colourful past.

Situated on Stubbs Island, in Clayoquot Sound, the former trading post dates back only a century and some ago, although Clayoquot (originally Wickaninnish) Sound has been occupied by Indians for untold centuries. Stubbs Island, situated off Tofino, does not seem to have attracted white habitation until 1875, when a Captain Pinney decided that it would be the ideal location for a trading post, the sound's first.

Outfitted with an array of ship chandlery and trade goods, he set up shop, convinced that passing shipmasters would be delighted to avail themselves of his merchandise. To attract their attention, and to assure them safe passage, Pinney built a beacon at the end of the island's long sandspit. Consisting of an elevated iron basket, which he loaded with firewood during the day and lit each evening, he sat back to await the inevitable flood of customers.

But few ships came. Perhaps their masters were afraid to risk entering the sound, despite Pinney's beacon. (Lennard Island lighthouse now serves this purpose.) Meanwhile, the Indians who did call were of little value as customers — they lacked both the need for such hardware as a ship's anchor, and the money with which to buy it in the first place.

Disheartened, and broke, Captain Pinney moved on, his store passing into the hands of an adventurous Victorian, Thomas Earle. Upon moving in, one of Earle's first moves was to sell most of his predecessor's inventory as scrap metal. He

seems to have developed some trade, probably with local natives, as he managed to hold on for some years before selling out to a Victoria firm, Stockham and Dawley. Previously, these partners had established a small post only a mile away, on an island near the Opitisaht village.

By this time, others were showing interest in Clayoquot Sound, particularly at Tofino, the region attracting the attention of prospectors and members of the famous sealing fleet. Because the sealers hired native hunters, the end of each season meant that many of the sound's original inhabitants had money and could buy goods and supplies at the partners' store.

The resulting trade prompted construction of a two-storey hotel. With its typical Old West false front, this building was the largest structure in what was fast becoming a small village. A photograph, taken some time after the turn of the century, shows a row of six or seven buildings on the beach, the largest of which is the Clayoquot Hotel. Eventually, Walter T. Dawley bought out partner Thomas Stockham's share of the business and operated the hotel and store until his retirement in 1937. Dawley also served as the mining recorder for the Clayoquot Mining District. Son-in-law Pierre Malon carried on the business a further four years, then sold the operation to partners Betty Farmer and her sister, Josephine Brydges.

"The original Clayoquot store was rather unusual," the late George Nicholson wrote in 1964. "Indians were not permitted inside. Instead, they had to make their purchases (mostly in trade) through a small wicket, handy to which the storekeeper

(for many years Frederick Christian Thornberg, a Dane) kept a loaded rifle. At times, when the Indians found the store closed, they displayed their wrath by firing buckshot at the closed porthole."

The disgruntled gunmen never hit their mark and storekeeper Thornberg survived to establish his own trading post at Ahousat. When demolished years afterward, the Clayoquot store's timbers were found to be liberally peppered with tiny holes — the result of buckshot, not termites.

For many years after 1901, Walter Dawley's brother Clarence ran the store. Walter was something of a character and, it would seem, a sucker for a bargain. According to Nicholson, he would make occasional buying trips to Victoria, then return to Clayoquot, laden down with treasure. Unfortunately, being out of touch with contemporary fashions as he was, he invariably loaded up on metropolitan Victoria's castoffs. As late as 1925, when Nicholson resided on the island, the store's attic was crammed with these discount purchases, all from a bygone era.

"There was black powder and buckshot by the hundred-weight, wads, percussion caps and wooden ramrods, all for the muzzleloaders which the Indians used to shoot fur seals with though by law they were supposed to use harpoons. Piled high were boxes of button-up and elastic-sided boots and patent leather dress shoes with pointed toes. Broad-rimmed men's felt hats, long out of style, bell-bottom pants and other articles of clothing. . .most of it subsequently found its way back to Victoria — sold to a fancy costume dealer."

The lone policeman of the Indian Department lived in the village, his house serving double duty as the lock-up. A provincial police constable's office was also located here, as were the post office, courthouse, mining recorder's office, and registrar of births, death and marriages.

In later years, Clayoquot, for all its isolation, became successful as a year-round resort (duck and geese hunters favoured it in winter). Clayoquot's enduring popularity would indicate that Captain Pinney was, literally, ahead of his time. ♣

(Top) Walter Dawley's hotel at Clayoquot.
(Above) View of Quachin Indian village and totem pole, Clayoquot.
(Opposite page, top) The west coast of Vancouver Island near Tofino.
(Opposite page, bottom) Two views of Clayoquot Inn, Clayoquot, 1978.
(Below left) Sandy beach at Clayoquot.
(Below centre) Thomas Earle, Victoria's pioneer merchant who took over Pinney's store at Clayoquot.
(Below right) Walter T. Dawley, trader and fur buyer at Clayoquot for over 40 years.

MAP #7 N

17. CLAYOQUOT
18. FORT DEFIANCE
19. PORT HUGHES

VARGAS IS.

MEARES IS.

TOFINO

PACIFIC OCEAN

LONG BEACH

KENNEDY LAKE

UCLUELET

(Below) Carpenter George Davidson's painting of Fort Defiance, Adventure Cove, showing the Columbia *moored off the fort, and the sloop* Adventure *on the ways. At the bottom Captain Gray is giving instructions to Mr. Yendell.*

FOR almost 200 years historians had pondered the mystery of Capt. Robert Gray's Fort Defiance. According to the records, the famous Boston trader had wintered in a sheltered cove in Clayoquot Sound while he repaired his ship and built a second, smaller craft. But just where his little camp, Fort Defiance, was situated remained a mystery until 1966 when an amateur archaeologist playing seaborne detective at last solved the clues to the long-sought Adventure Cove.

This intriguing puzzle began in 1791, when Gray, in command of the trading vessel *Columbia,* returned to the Pacific Northwest for his second trading cruise in two years. Throughout the summer, the 220-ton *Columbia* bartered sundry goods for prime sea otter pelts. But, unlike her previous voyage, the *Columbia* carried more in her holds than trading trinkets, Gray having brought with him the timbers, stern post and stem for construction of a sloop which he planned to use in shallow waters, as well as 2,000 handmade bricks for ballast.

To build this sloop he required a favourable launching site. The location he finally chose was Clickscleuctsee, a cove "form'd by an Isle and the SE shore Clioquot sound, so small that when the ship was moor'd you might throw a stone upon

the beach in any direction." The entrance to this secluded cove was only a hundred feet wide. But its waters were deep enough for the *Columbia* to be moored (hawsers securing her to trees on the shore), safe from storm, while on the smooth beach, the ship's company could lay the sloop's keel.

In his diary, Lieut. John Boit, the 16-year-old fifth officer, described the finding of the cove and their landing. On September 19, 1791, he wrote: "Captain Gray went with two longboats up the sound for to seek a convenient cove. In the evening the Capt. returned having found a place to his mind 1 league from where the ship lay." The next day, the *Columbia* "weigh'd with light airs and with the long boats ahead, assisted by the brig's crew we tow'd and sail'd into winter quarters which we call'd Adventure Cove, and moor'd the ship for the winter. Vast many of the natives alongside and appeared pleas'd with the idea of our tarrying with them for the cold season."

Despite the Indians' apparent friendliness, Gray ordered his 50 men to build a sturdy log house which he named Fort Defiance. First Mate Robert Haswell was placed in command of several seamen and all of the "mechanics," the rest remaining aboard the *Columbia.* Although the fort lacked both bastions and palisades, it earned its title by the fact that it was armed with two cannon and its walls were loop-holed for muskets.

Some 36 feet by 18 feet in size, the two-storey structure was chinked with mortar made from burnt shells and clay. The upper floor, with a loft large enough to build small boats, was finished with cedar planking traded with local Indians for scraps of iron. For heat and cooking purposes there was a large brick fireplace, a second being used as a forge. Outside the "fort" were a blacksmith shop and forge, two saw pits and a carpenter's shed roofed with tree boughs.

There, under constant surveillance by natives, Gray's men worked on the 45-ton sloop and its whaleboat, the latter being built upstairs in the fort, and occupying the shipwrights' attention when inclement weather halted work on the sloop outside. Despite having to keep a careful watch on their neighbours, the traders made rapid progress and word of their project spread throughout the tribes. Among those who came to view the sloop under construction, and to marvel at how the whites intended to move it to the water's edge, was the powerful Chief Wickanninish. Other visitors were not as friendly or as interested in the fine art of shipbuilding and, more than once, Gray's men found it necessary to fire warning shots to keep them under control.

Although the Americans had brought some parts for the sloop from Boston, it was necessary to utilize many local materials, such as the tallest, straightest fir and cedar trees they could find in the area. Floated back to the fort, the logs were hauled into position over the two saw pits, where seamen sweated at the laborious task of whipsawing them into planks.

It was hard, monotonous work and the men, a continent away from home, suffered keenly from their isolation. Thus, on Christmas Day, 1791, the lonely adventurers celebrated British Columbia's first yuletide "with as much circumstance and hilarity as it was possible to do in simulation of the manner of honoring it in New England.

"At dawn the men were astir," wrote the late provincial historian B.A. McKelvie. "They hastened ashore from the vessel, and out of the fort, to the nearby woods and gathered great armfuls of evergreen; searched for deciduous leaves that still bore the flaming colors of the late autumn, and the berries that continued to grow. With laughter and merriment — and often a bit of strained boisterousness when thoughts arose of how their kin were doing similar work that day on the other side of the continent — the Columbia and Fort Defiance were soon decorated for the occasion. Flags and bunting of the vessel add(ed) to the color of the scene. . . ."

Once carpenters had finished erecting a large frame on which the necessary number of spits could be suspended over a roaring fire, 20 fat and succulent geese were basted over the flames, as others turned to the equally mouthwatering task of unloading the required kegs of rum and other liquors from the ship under the careful eye of Robert Haswell. Upon the arrival of their guests, Chief Wickanninish and his royal court, Captain Gray and his officers greeted the entourage with due pomp and ceremony on the beach, and gave the visitors a tour of the ship and shore installations.

Then all turned to the banquet; a repast worthy of kings, recorded the Columbia's supercargo, John Hoskins. The piece de resistance, he said, was a giant "whortleberry" (huckleberry) pudding which, with the 20 geese, was soon devoured, along with generous quantities of liquid refreshment. As native custom forbade the attendance of women,

the poor ladies had to wait all the while in the canoes! They were not totally forgotten, however, the considerate Wickanninish detailing slaves to carry an occasional titbit to the gentler sex.

Diner finished, there were toasts to the president of the United States, singing, games and, "merriment galore." Remarkably, as supercargo Hoskins was quick to point out, the event was not marred by a single instance of intoxication, all being careful to observe his own limit.

With midnight, it was over. After firing a salute with the Columbia's guns, the lights were extinguished and everyone retired. The province's first Christmas party was history.

Not to be outdone, Chief Wickanninish marked New Year's Day with a party of his own, several of the white traders being invited to attend. On January 1, 1792, a crew under the command of Lieutenant Boit rowed the "jolly boat" to the village and made their way to the chieftain's long house, which was crowded with visitors from neighbouring tribes. "As soon as the king saw me," recounted the young lieutenant, "I was called toward him, and seated upon his right. This house was about 80 feet long, and 40 broad, and about 18 feet high with a flat roof. The king was elevated about two feet higher than the company with a canopy over his head, stuck full of animals' teeth. The company consisted of above 100 men, all considerably advanced in years. . . .

"The entertainment (probably a concoction of fish spawn, berries and oil) was served up in wooded bowls. . . I was invited strongly to partake, but the smell was enough — therefore pleaded indisposition. . . The king informed me there was going to be a dance in the evening, and wished me to stay. However, I declined, and returned on board."

On March 21, tragedy struck the little company with the death of bosun Benjamin Harding, who after a brief service, was buried near the blockhouse. The next day the Adventure, as the sloop had been christened, was launched, Boit recording that the operation went "admirably." Within two days, rigged and ready for sea, she was placed under command of Captain Haswell and a crew of 10. Proudly, Boit described the Adventure as "one of the prettiest vessels I ever saw, of about 45 tons, with handsome figure head and false badges, and other ways touched off in high style. There was not a butt either in the planks on deck or sides, and the planks not above nine inches high. Victualled for four months cruise and supplied with articles for the Queen Charlotte Islands trade."

No sooner was the sloop completed, than Captain Gray ordered Boit to lead an attack against the nearby village of "Opitisaht." According to his diary, Boit was less than enthused by the assignment, writing: "I am sorry to be under the necessity of remarking that this day I was sent with three boats all well mann'd and armed to destroy the village of Opitsatah. It was a command I was in no ways tenacious of, and am grieved to think that Captain Gray should let his passion go so far.

"The village was about half a mile in diameter, and contained upwards of 200 houses generally well built for Indian. Every door that you entered was in resemblance to a human and beast head and carved from solid logs, the passageway being through the mouth, besides which there was much carved work about the dwellings of which was by no means inelegant. This fine village, the work of ages, was totally destroyed."

Two weeks before, some visiting chieftains had been observed in the act of speaking with a boy who had joined the Columbia in the Sandwich Islands. Suspicious, Gray had questioned the lad, who admitted that the Indians had asked him

(Far left) Capt. Robert Gray.
(Left) Capt. Robert Haswell commanded the newly-built Adventure.

(Opposite page, top) Discoverer Ken Gibson digs for proof that this cove was the site of Captain Gray's winter quarters in Clayoquot Sound.
(Opposite page, right) An aerial view of Adventure Cove.
(Opposite page, bottom) This Ahousat woven hat is similar to the ones worn by the natives of Clayoquot Sound.

(Below) An aerial view of the west coast of Vancouver Island near Tofino.

(Above left) Searching for hidden clues at Adventure Cove.
(Above right) Some of the thousands of pieces of old, handmade bricks recovered at Adventure Cove. Subsequent tests by experts verified that these probably were shipped as ballast aboard the sailing ship Columbia 200 years ago.
(Below) Adventure Cove, as photographed from the same spot in which Davidson drew the original of Fort Defiance. Chief clue was the row of hills in the background.

to wet the whites' powder and to steal shot for the natives. As the *Columbia* had been on the ways for graving, it had been a tense situation. Gray had ordered his men to proceed with the job with all possible speed, although an attack seemed imminent. That night, several canoe loads of warriors had appeared in the inlet and begun "hooping." The alarmed whites, all armed, had maintained a vigilant lookout until morning, when work on the *Columbia* was completed and she was refloated. By March 4 she was fully rigged, with her hold stowed and ready to sail.

On the eve of the whites' departure from the area, Captain Gray had given the order to destroy the village as reprisal.

Then the *Columbia* sailed away to the south, Gray discovering the mighty river which he named after his ship, before proceeding to China and home and becoming master of the first American ship to circumnavigate the globe. Before leaving the Northwest he had sold the *Adventure* to the Spanish for 72 prime otter pelts (about $4,000).

With the traders' departure under such unhappy cir-

cumstances, the site of short-lived Fort Defiance was lost to history, its destruction believed to have been hastened by Gray's order to strip it of all salvageable articles, and by vengeful natives.

Historians long pondered the exact location of Gray's winter quarters. But it was not until the summer of 1966 that the search for Fort Defiance was concluded by a young Tofino resident, Ken Gibson, and an interested group of fishermen, loggers and contractors. Working from a handful of clues provided by the *Columbia's* log, and Lieutenant Boit's diary, they pinpointed Adventure Cove's position on the western shore of Meares Island. That December the lieutenant-governor of the province of British Columbia approved an order-in-council formally recognizing that "the remains of Fort Defiance, the winter quarters of Robert Gray in the years 1791-1792, have been located on lands situated on the west coast of Vancouver Island in the vicinity of Lemmens Inlet." The site was placed under the Archaeological and Historic Sites Protection Act.   ♣

Port Hughes

MOST Vancouver Island communities have grown over the years. Some, like Leechtown, Mount Sicker and Cassidy, have vanished. Others, such as Extension and Union Bay, survive, although as shadows of their former glory.

Some disappeared almost before they started. Port Hughes, Clayoquot district, was such a "town." Situated at the head of Bedwell Sound, at the mouth of Bedwell (then Bear) River, it "assumed very considerable proportions" in August, 1899, when the *Colonist* reported that it had become the headquarters of more than 60 mines in the region.

The west coast of Vancouver Island was experiencing a mining boom at the turn of the century, particularly in the mountains behind Bedwell Inlet. From the miners' viewpoint Port Hughes was ideally located, the new townsite having been so positioned that, unlike other west coast settlements, it "absolutely controls the tributary mining district — its business is not divided or scattered." To link the town and mines a road and seven bridges had been built.

Six weeks later it was reported that former Victoria alderman Moses McGregor had returned to Victoria from the "new and growing town of Port Hughes," where he had supervised the building of a 14-room hotel, which he expected to open in three weeks. McGregor pointed out that Port Hughes now enjoyed regular mail service and its potential had been enhanced by the discovery of yet another gold mine.

Optimism was high: "All the mines on the West Coast are booming," reported the Victoria daily, "not in the undesirable American sense but in the healthiest acceptance of the term. . . (Most of those involved) still believe that the future great city of British Columbia will be in their immediate neighborhood. . . Great activity is noted at Port Hughes, Clayoquot, Hayes (Landing), Alberni — in fact every mining point in the district; while the salmon industry is also proving up. . . ."

At Quatsino a coal mine had been pushed to the 140-foot level, and the discovery of ledges of copper in the locality added to the widespread belief that Vancouver Island's neglected west coast was a second Kootenay and on the verge of long-term prosperity.

Bedwell Sound and "Bear" River originally attracted the attention of gold miners in the 1860s, during the Leech River excitement. Almost a quarter of a century after, 15 Chinese prospectors tried washing for gold on the upper reaches of the river. According to provincial assayer Herbert Carmichael, they "suddenly left in a body, having been driven away, it is said, by superstitious fears engendered by the sudden death of one of their number. The workings of these early miners are still visible (1899) and it is reported that they found considerable gold, but that the numerous large boulders prevented the workings being profitable."

At the height of mining activity in this region the main trail from Port Hughes led to the Seattle, New York, Castle, Galena, Corona and Belvidere properties. The Corona group reported assays running from $18 to $200 in gold per ton.

The area marked time until 1912, when the Big Interior group of claims, a more recent development, was bought by

The Buccaneer mine on the Bedwell River, during its first day of operation.

an English company. The richness of the copper ores prompted H.H. Johnson, Victoria representative for Ptarmigan Mines Limited, to establish a camp at the mouth of the river. This would indicate that, even then, Port Hughes had failed.

Seven weeks after development work began in 1914, the outbreak of the First World War prompted every employee to enlist and operations were suspended. In this brief period six tunnels had been started, a further mile and a quarter of road completed through difficult terrain, and a large bridge built across the Bear River. By the following year mining in the area resumed. The main obstacle to development, despite the exceptional value of the copper ores found here, was its inaccessibility.

In 1919 Ptarmigan's chief engineer Johnson returned from active service and made a quick visit to the mine site. Because it had been left without even a caretaker, most of the equipment was badly rusted or ruined, including the tramway which had been salvaged from the Tyee Mine at Mount Sicker, and one and a half tons of explosives which had been left exposed to the elements. Even the hard-won road to the mine was in poor repair.

It was 1926 before Ptarmigan Mines, under the direction of the Earl of Denbigh, refinanced and prepared to start all over. Others in this region had suffered misfortune, J.H. Woodworth and associates, who had placer claims at the head of Bedwell River, having lost their mill and camp to fire in the fall of 1922. In 1928 some work on the Ptarmigan property was in progress as "reports would indicate that (it) is favorable for extensive development." The annual mines report for 1930 notes that the wagon road from Bedwell Sound was impassable.

Interest in the Clayoquot mining division was rekindled in 1933 by the discovery of gold-bearing quartz veins at the head of Herbert Inlet, immediately to the west of Bedwell Sound. Small-scale mining continued throughout this region until the 1960s. ♣

Clo-oose

A metropolis by the sea. Such, years ago, was a promoter's fanciful picture of the little Indian village of Clo-oose. Although few who have visited this former fishing settlement, situated midway between Port Renfrew and Bamfield on Vancouver Island's southwestern coast, would dispute the area's rugged grandeur and sparkling beaches, they would take issue with this earlyday shyster's portrayal of Clo-oose (Indian for "a safe landing") as a booming seaport with large docking facilities for ships of the world, of wide streets and substantial buildings. . . .

It was, alas, all a lie. Clo-oose was then, and is now, no more than an isolated waypoint which faces the open Pacific. Even the few residents that it had are gone, including those unfortunate enough to have fallen for, and invested in, this bogus development scheme of long past.

At the turn of the century, the lower Vancouver Island rain forests were attracting hundreds of settlers from two continents, and from every walk of life. Lured by glowing promotional reports of the Island's rain forests as the last frontier of virgin soil, where one could grow potatoes the size of footballs and corn as tall as trees, many families abandoned the comforts of the Old Country and city for the dubious joys of homesteading on distant Vancouver Island. Even the provincial government was guilty of misrepresentation, blithely promising roads and services that were never delivered. The result for many of these settlers was, as at Cape Scott, hardship and poverty. Finally, their spirits broken by a merciless wilderness which fought them every inch of the way, and with all of their savings gone, they returned to "civilization" and a more prosaic, if more secure, way of life. Their homesteads, for which they had given blood, sweat and tears, were soon reclaimed by the jungle-thick salal and forests.

So it had been at Cape Scott, and so it was at Clo-oose.

If Clo-oose failed to hold its pioneers, it has succeeded in holding the hearts of many who, even today, recall their stay there with some affection.

At first, of course, Clo-oose seemed to be almost everything that its promoters had claimed it to be. To the east, in Vancouver Island's interior, the Canadian National Railway (CNR) was pushing its way northward to Lake Cowichan and plans for a spur to Clo-oose, which would at last link the Island's magnificent west coast by rail to the rest of the province, were widely touted. Regular steamship service had already been inaugurated, the faithful Ss *Tees* and *Princess Maquinna* delivering cargoes of lumber and building materials, as, on the Prairies, and in the Old Country, high pressure salesman spun incredible tales of an idyllic life by the sea.

From Victoria, the West Coast Development Company ferried prospective buyers to and from its subdivisions at Clo-oose by its own launch, the *Enilada,* where they were wined and dined at the Bungalow Inn. But most sales were made at long distance, to people who signed on the dotted line without having seen their new homesteads. Accepting the salesmen at their words, these buyers paid hard cash for lots that were no more than lines on a chart; for waterfront properties that turned out to be below the high-water mark; for waterfront lots that in actuality were landlocked by other properties; and for "ocean-view" land from which they could not see the sea.

Some, of course, realized their mistake the minute they set

(Opposite page) Clo-oose. More than half a century after unscrupulous real estate promoters depicted this fishing village as a bustling city, it remains as isolated as ever. (Top inset) The Clo-oose cemetery. (Bottom inset) Mrs. Ross with some of the children of her Sunday school class at Clo-oose in 1930. The ungainly two-storey structure in the background is the Indian hall.
(Below) Pulling a log up the beach at Clo-oose, 1930.

eyes on the settlement from the decks of the coastal steamers, and, sadder but wiser, went right back home. Others, although shocked when they found neither dock nor township, had no choice but to make the best of it, having sold everything they had to come to Clo-oose. Yet others had brought everything with them, from family heirloom to grand piano.

Temporarily establishing their families in the beach-side "Tent City," the head of the household went to work with axe, shovel and back. For many the realities of pre-empting (the Canadian euphemism for homesteading) came soon, and the resolve to battle the rain forest soon faltered. Others, of stronger stuff, built sturdy cabins of log and driftwood and cleared something in the way of a farm, complete with gardens and produce. However, despite the obvious fertility of the soil, the heavy annual rainfall and omnipresent fog discouraged growth of some of the more desirable crops.

Each Saturday night, on "steamboat day," and on special occasions, there were community dances and get-togethers, made all the more intimate by a sense of isolation and independence from the outside world. In summer months the small population of Nitinaht Indians swelled with the arrival of the fishing fleet which called there for supplies and unloaded their catches at the busy Lummy Bay Packing Company at Nitinat Narrows.

The Nitinahts had long settled here, the village apparently having boasted as many as 400 warriors; if correct this would have indicated a total population of about 1,000 persons. By the turn of the century smallpox and other factors had reduced the Nitinaht band, famous for its whale hunting exploits, to 200. With the advent of sealing as a vast, international industry, many of these former warriors found ready employment aboard the sealing schooners which ranged as far as Bering Sea in their annual hunts. By the 1920s salmon fishing had replaced this dangerous occupation as the prime source of employment; then this too was superseded by logging.

During Prohibition Clo-oose became popular as a haven for the rum-running fleet which operated between British Columbia and California, and it is local legend that the lady proprietor of the Clo-oose general store became wealthy by catering to this trade. With all of this activity had come brief prosperity for the village as a whole — and the provincial police when general drunkenness led to violence.

Perhaps the first real sign that dreams of a "metropolitan" Clo-oose were not to be fulfilled had been the CNR's decision not to push on to Nitinat, let alone to the little west coast settlement. Only the maintenance of the famous "Life-saving Trail," nearby logging operations, and some fishing and trapping provided employment on a steadily declining basis. Slowly the forest won, as the pioneers lost faith and drifted back to the world beyond Vancouver Island's lonely southwestern coast. When the cannery shut down the fishermen no longer called and the population dwindled with each passing year.

During the Second World War, four of the last seven white families moved away. In 1952 the last regular link with the outer world, the faithful old *Princess Maquinna,* was retired. This was the final blow, and everyone except several Indian families, a missionary and a lineman who serviced the telephone line, packed up and left.

"In 1953," longtime resident Jim Hamilton wrote in a Victoria newspaper, "the daughter of one of the early visitors returned to the area with her husband and family. The missionary and lineman retired to the cities in due course and it fell to she

(sic) and her husband and son to carry on the post office and to maintain the telephone lines and trails in the vicinity.

"In 1956 Moore-Whittington commenced logging on the Nitinat and several of the Indian families gravitated to this operation and in 1964 it was decided by the Department of Indian Affairs to move their people to a reserve at the north end of Nitinat at the termination point of the road to Lake Cowichan and Port Alberni."

By this time only five native families were involved. The remaining white family held on until the summer of 1966. On August 11, the post office of Clo-oose was formally closed, and with it, a fascinating, somewhat sad chapter in Vancouver Island history.

To say that Clo-oose is gone is not to say that it is forgotten. Many remember the little settlement, particularly the unique way in which the steamers had landed passengers and freight there. Despite all that the real estate promoters said to the contrary, there never was so much as a wharf. Clo-oose faced the vast open Pacific and ships of any size could not anchor there much of the time. Bad weather, in fact, had been one of the unhappier facts of life for Clo-oose residents for, when the winds blew, the steamers could not stop. As the *Maquinna* and her earlier sisters called at 10-day intervals, storms could mean a long wait for supplies; Christmas often came late for the settlers, it being some time in January before winter storms abated enough to let them receive their holiday freight.

Only when the seas were glassy smooth did the *Maquinna* drop anchor. Usually, at such times, she eased in as close to shore as possible. Her master would then turn her into the broad swells, bow-on, and hold her in position by keeping her under way. Then a flotilla of dugout canoes would push off from the beach, come alongside the cargo doors, which were just above sea level, and load freight and passengers for the run to shore. This was always a delicate manoeuvre for both shipmaster and boatman, as an unexpected roll of the ship could result in the hold being flooded, and disaster for the man in the canoe alongside.

"Tourists marvelled at the way such frail craft were manipulated," George Nicholson explained in *Vancouver Island's West Coast.* Usually the canoes were handled by "one old Indian with a short paddle," as a younger native squatted in the stern to catch the freight as it was thrown from the ship. "Occasionally a passenger bound for Clo-oose had to be taken ashore the same way and if it happened to be a nervous person, or a woman, camera-armed tourists got a greater thrill.

"Watching the heavily-laden canoes go ashore was just as exciting, especially as they neared the beach, where, regardless of how the sea appeared to be, the swells always broke. More so when it was really rough and a ducking for someone and wet freight usually resulted."

Nicholson also paid tribute to the grand old man of Clo-oose, David Logan, for years the area's postmaster, telephone lineman, storekeeper, justice of the peace and all-round handyman. Probably more than any other man, Logan knew first hand the horrors of shipwreck along this dangerous shore. Born in Leith, Scotland, Logan migrated to the United States with his parents at the age of four, and arrived on Vancouver Island as a young husband to work in the Wellington mines after experience as an iron miner and farmer. In 1904 he was hired to take charge of a herd of cattle on the Cheewhat (originally called "Chockwheat") River, at Clo-oose. This was during the halcyon era when people were yet confident of the west coast's potential as an agricultural El Dorado, and such cattle-raising experiments had already been conducted at several other west coast Island points. But, Nicholson notes, the country "was never suited for this or any other kind of farming." Before long Logan found himself unemployed — there being no cattle left to manage!

Undaunted, the hardy young Scotsman built a home on the beach and opened a store, sold groceries and acted as postmaster and justice of the peace. He also patrolled a 25-mile section of the "one-wire, tree-to-tree telephone line that extended from Cape Beale," which had to be kept open at all times in the event of shipwreck. Just how important this position was is evidenced by the fact that, between the years 1904-38, 20 major shipwrecks, involving great loss of life and property, occurred along this jagged stretch of coast; eight of them occurred in Logan's jurisdiction. It was the lineman's job to do his best at rescuing survivors, or help in the grim task of finding and burying the dead.

Another memorable Clo-oose resident was Jacob Chipps, a native Indian whose act of heroism and human endurance must be unparalleled to this day.

In July 1907, Chipps, his 18-year-old daughter Ida, her infant of 18 months, and three companions were off Vancouver's Point Grey, bound for the Fraser River fishing grounds. A heavy swell rocked the Strait of Georgia that afternoon, and their little boat heaved drunkenly. Chipps was in the stern, steering, when the baby began to cry. Turning slightly to see what was the matter, he released his grip on the tiller. His careless move came at the precise moment that a mountainous wave streaked down upon them. Before he could regain control the boat was swept onto its side and its six occupants pitched into the frigid sea.

Chipps and three passengers managed to cling to the upturned boat's keel but his daughter, baby still clutched tightly to her breast, was carried beyond reach. Upon seeing her danger Chipps stripped off his clothes and boots, including his money-belt which contained $700, and swam to his daughter's side.

Grabbing her with one arm, the baby in the other, Chipps, described as being "a magnificent specimen of manhood, strong, powerful and skilful," began swimming back to the boat. But that craft, with its helpless passengers, was hurled away by the wind, leaving the frightened grandfather with his unconscious charges miles from shore and facing certain death.

Jacob Chipps could not remember what happened after that. He knew only that he struggled ashore at midnight. His companions, who had been rescued, estimated that they had been capsized at 5 p.m., meaning that Chipps had been in the water seven hours!

Rescuers who found the exhausted Indian lying, seemingly lifeless, on the beach, marvelled at the nightmare he had endured. They could only imagine what he had been through. Somehow, daughter and grandchild wrapped his his arms, he had dog-paddled the several miles to shore. How many hours he swam, virtually unconscious, is beyond knowing. Blindly, he had struggled onward, ever onward, driven by a super-human compulsion to save his family.

When revived the valiant Chipps had asked of his daughter and her baby. Unfortunately, they were beyond help, having died of exposure, probably within half an hour of the accident.

Days later the CPR steamer Princess Victoria brought a solemn Chipps and the bodies of Ida and her baby to Victoria for burial. The grieving fisherman vowed he would never again live at Clo-oose, "where there are so many things to remind him of his lost ones." The following month, Jacob Chipps was awarded the Royal Humane Society Medal for his remarkable feat.

More recently another Clo-oose resident, Sybil Hardwick, told a Vancouver Sun reporter of her treasured memories of long-ago Clo-oose. Miss Hardwick was 11 years old when she and her family moved to the lonely village where, with her younger brother, she spent the days "tearing along the long, sandy beach. . .screaming with the sheer joy of the pounding sounds of the breakers. . . It's a marvellous country. I would trade all the modern gadgets of today's society for the good times I had there in my youth."

Not all of her memories were happy ones. It had been Sybil Hardwick who first discovered the wreck of the barquentine Skagit when it ran aground near Nitinat and Clo-oose, in 1906. Two of the ship's company, the cook and a seaman, died in the stranding. Miss Hardwick watched the peremptory burial service of the cook, whose shipmates had simply dropped his body into the sea "head first like a limp doll." On a nearby cliff, a number of wailing Indian women expressed their grief for the lost sailors.

Known to local Indians, who continued to wear little more than loin cloths and Hudson's Bay blankets, as "Cloosh tenash Klootchman" — "good little woman" — because of her skill at weaving Indian blankets, the young Miss Hardwick had also mastered the native dialect. Her father, a former minister and gold miner, first arrived at Clo-oose in 1906 as a timber cruiser, the family having travelled from Princeton by pack train, and then aboard the little ship Tees. "There was no pier at Clo-oose," she said "so we went ashore by climbing down a rope ladder into a canoe." As one had to very carefully time their jump from the swinging rope to the swaying canoe, it was, to say the least, a precarious mode of disembarkation and, more than once, ill-fated. Once, she recalled, a missionary's wife had had to swim ashore unaided when she missed her "step" into a waiting canoe.

Once ashore, the family had moved into the large house occupied by Rev. Charles Docksteader and his family. The home has since vanished before the onslaught of wind and wave. Up until recent years a handful of houses and the old church on the point had survived at Clo-oose, two being used for a summer resort. By 1970 the others were in a sad state of repair, their unpainted and silvered walls all that remained of happier days at Clo-oose. Of the old cannery only a few rows of slime-green pilings showed where it once stood. One house had a permanent occupant, Joshua Edgar, an aged member of the Nitinaht band who was born, married and raised his family there. When the others moved away Joshua remained with his memories.

Unlike other Vancouver Island ghost towns, Clo-oose has some hope for the future. The spectacular scenery to be found here has become known to hundreds who have hiked the old shipwreck trail.

Even today access to Clo-oose is restricted to travel by logging road and boat, chartered plane or, the hard way, by hiking along the West Coast Trail. All who have made the trip swear that it is well worth the effort, the gently curving beach at Clo-oose being rated as equal to those of the South Pacific. Although Clo-oose will never become a metropolis, or even live again as a community, it will continue to live on in the hearts of all fortunate enough to have resided or visited here, a fitting monument for any community. ♣

Kildonan

UCHUCKLESIT Inlet (the name is derived from the Indian word, *how-chuck-les-aht* — "people who live by a spring situated on or at the end of a deep inlet") next experienced the dubious blessings of progress in 1903 when captains Macdonald and Ternan established the Alberni Packing Company, midway along the sheltered inlet's southeastern shore.

Seven years later Wallace Brothers Packing Company acquired the plant and the site was named Kildonan, after their Scottish hometown. Upon reorganization as Wallace Fisheries, just before the First World War, a cold storage plant was built to engage in the fresh and frozen fish trade. Because the cannery was built at the foot of a steep mountain-side the entire development sat on pilings.

The "island" settlement boomed in 1925 when the mysterious pilchard (*sardinops caerules*), bigger brother of the herring, suddenly appeared in abundance in British Columbia waters. "...The waters adjacent to the west coast of Vancouver Island," wrote George Nicholson, in *Vancouver Island's West Coast,* "appeared to be literally alive with them; schools acres in extent were frequently observed.

"For years previously the sardine industry on the California coast had been in full swing. A percentage of the catch, by U.S. law, had to be canned for human consumption, the balance processed into meal and oil. Coincidentally with an

The MV **Lady Rose.** *The Bill Maximick painting below shows her making her way through Alberni Canal. At right she is unloading freight at Kildonan.*

96 Ghost Towns & Mining Camps of B.C.

increased demand for these latter products for agriculture and manufacturing purposes, it was discovered that the pilchard found off our coast was the same fish, only considerably larger. Also, that grown to maturity, its oil content was far greater in proportion to its size than when caught farther south as a sardine."

British Columbia fishermen needed no prompting.

The next three years were reminiscent of the gold stampede which opened the provincial hinterland three-quarters of a century before. Twenty-six pilchard reduction plants — costing as much as $250,000 each — blossomed in the hundred-odd miles between Kyuquot and Barkley Sound. A thousand men operated the busy plants and more than 200 seiners, tugs and scows during the four-and-a-half-month season.

Sites for the reduction plants had been at a premium, Major Nicholson recalled. Prime requisites were "good penetration for pile-driving, shelter for boats and docks, and above all, a plentiful water supply."

Kildonan qualified on all counts and its owners immediately joined in the rush, at the height of which, "Construction crews could ask any price for their hire. Victoria and Vancouver shipyards worked night and day building seine boats and scows, while fishing companies vied with one another in a mad scramble to cash in on the bonanza. Meanwhile the pilchards continued to show up in greater bulk."

Millions of the valuable pilchard were hauled, squirming, into the seiners' nets, to be hustled ashore by scow, during the first three years. Then the unusual visitor from the south offered his first surprise: from his favourite sheltered waters, Kyuquot, Nootka, Clayoquot and Barkley Sounds, the pilchard moved out — a long way out.

This change of habit caused the fishermen no little confusion at first, not to mention expense. The smaller seiners which had reaped such rich harvests in the inlets could not brave the heavy swells of the open sea, nor could the flat-bottomed scows. This meant bigger seiners and 100-ton packers.

Consequently the smaller plants could not compete. Within 15 years 16 had closed shop. The surviving giants — among them Kildonan — had but a few seasons left.

Then. . .almost as dramatically as they had first appeared in provincial waters, the pilchard vanished. After a fairly light harvest (15,000 tons) in 1944, fishermen returned to port again and again, having sailed as far south as Oregon, with light or empty holds. In 1949 only 67 tons of meal were produced. It was not enough; the last reduction plants closed and a $2 million industry was dead.

The cannery and reduction plant at Kildonan, which had been acquired from the British Columbia Fishing and Packing Company by British Columbia Packers in 1928, survived the loss of the pilchard. After the Second World War British Columbia Packers began to collect fish with packers and send them to their Imperial Cannery at Steveston. The Kildonan reduction plant continued to operate during the herring season until 1960 and the ice-making plant served fishermen for a further two years. During its heyday as a cannery, Kildonan's main products were sockeye and chum salmon, pilchard and herring fish meal and oil. Between 1903 and 1950 more than a million cases of canned products were shipped out of Kildonan.

In 1962, run-down from neglect, the cannery buildings and wharves were demolished and burned. Just a single stucco house, a wharf and the bones of some of the old pilings remained of the settlement which, at the height of the pilchard season, often had 300 residents. Many marine charts yet in use show Kildonan as a fuelling depot; the *Gazetteer of Canada* lists Kildonan as a post office and steamer landing.   ♣

In 1962 the Kildonan cannery and wharves were demolished and burned. At the height of the pilchard season as many as 300 persons had worked here.

"We have an unlimited amount of ore in sight; we have the value; we have the greatest faculties possible, and we have, gentlemen, the prospects of the greatest mining camp in British Columbia."

— unidentified Alberni prospector, April 1897

☆ ☆ ☆

ANOTHER west coast mining camp with visions of greatness was Hayes Landing, or Port Hayes, on the west side of Alberni Canal, half a mile south of Nahmint Bay and 14 miles from Port Alberni. Under the supervision of Col. G.H. Hayes, the Nahmint Mining Company, of Portland, Oregon, was organized in 1898 with a capital of $100,000. That year they pushed 600 feet of tunnel on their four full-sized claims and three fractions near the mouth of the Nahmint River and shipped 120 tons of ore containing copper, gold and silver. Investments at the mine-site had been heavy, involving the building of a boarding house to accommodate 30 men, two ore sheds, wharf ("suitable for the largest vessels"), warehouse, office, manager's residence, storeroom, stable and smaller buildings. From the wharf a wagon road zigzagged for two miles up the steep mountain-side to the mine.

In March, 1899, it was reported in Victoria that: "There seems to be no doubt now that Hayes' mine, as it is popularly known, is one of the best properties in the province, and there are prospects that the five gentlemen who own it will reap rich harvests as the reward of their industry. Only recently a separate and distinct chute of rich ore was struck in the mine. The chute was struck 120 feet west of the body of ore on which the company has been at work, a drift having been run from the main tunnel. The new chute shows for 300 feet at the surface, and it is expected that it will continue that size. The *Queen City* will bring down between 30 and 50 tons of this ore for shipment to the Tacoma smelter on her next trip.

"So far the company has shipped 300 tons of ore from the mine, and the smelter returns have been most satisfactory. . .Speaking yesterday of the advisability of erecting a smelter for the treatment of the Island ores, Col. Hayes said the great trouble was the sameness of the ores, which would make it necessary to bring in some from other sections for fluxing purposes."

Less than three months later, Colonel Hayes and company faced an unexpected obstacle in the form of the provincial government, which had declared an eight-hour working day in the mining industry. When his men refused to accept less than their $3.50 per 10-hour shift for the shorter work day, Colonel Hayes ordered the mine shut down.

Agreement between management and the workers was ultimately reached as Gold Commissioner Thomas Fletcher subsequently described the Nahmint Company's operation as "by far the best developed property in the District, having over 1,000 feet of underground workings and employing an average of eight men underground and four above. . .A very considerable body of good chalcopyrite ore (copper) is exposed and

several shipments have been made this past year which, from smelter returns, ran about 10 to 12% copper with small values in gold and silver."

The following year the mine, known variously as the J.J.J., Three Jays, and the Hayes Mine, failed to ship any ore, although up to 30 men were steadily employed on the property. Previously, ores shipped to the Tacoma smelter had yielded an average return of 13 per cent copper, one and a-half ounces of silver and 65¢ in gold to the ton. Known ore reserves were promising and improvements at the mine-site included the construction of ore sheds, two blacksmiths shops and a shaft-house.

In 1901 the company chartered a steamer to ship its ore to Tacoma. By this time the underground workings had been pushed to almost a mile in length, a new compressor and boilers had been installed, a mile-long tramway capable of carrying 100 tons of ore per 24-hour shift constructed between the mine and wharf, and new powerhouse and terminal building completed. Throughout the year an average of 35 men had been employed in mining and development work.

Only two years later, after a quarter of a million dollars, and the shipment of 2,000 tons of eight per cent copper ore, the owner belatedly concluded that the ore was too low-grade to ship, ceased operations and placed their fine buildings, tramway and road under a watchman's care. In 1910 the caretaker was withdrawn, the buildings sold for salvage, the machinery dismantled, and the Crown-granted claims reverted to the provincial government for unpaid taxes. In the autumn of 1916 W.G. Tanner and associates of Seattle secured a lease on the property and proposed to reopen the mine and to treat the ore on the site by an oil-flotation process.

The Hayes group had been stymied by the fact that, the farther they had followed the mineralized veins, the lower the percentage of copper obtained. This, coupled with a low market price for that metal, transportation and smelter charges, had spelled doom for their ambitious efforts. The Tanner interests immediately began to clear out the old workings, rebuild the camp and reopen the roadway — all on the premise that a thorough prospecting of the property would prove it worthy of an on-site concentrator.

They were wrong.

In 1928 Alberni Mines Limited, incorporated with a capitalization of $2 million, obtained the historic property and some adjoining claims, and cleared out some of the original workings. Resident mining engineer George A. Clothier reported that their efforts had uncovered promising showings of chalcopyrite-bearing magnetite: "Altogether the property impresses me as being of considerable prospective merit, warranting considerable exploration."

The following year he had to report that, as far as he could learn, nothing had been done on the property since his last visit. ♣

Barclay Townsite

A salmon cannery at Barkley Sound, Vancouver Island. Barclay Townsite, Uchucklesit Inlet, at the entrance to Alberni Inlet, Barkley Sound, never amounted to more than a promoter's dream.

TWO attempts have been made to establish settlements on Uchucklesit Inlet, the landlocked harbour at the entrance to Alberni Inlet, Barkley Sound. The first, Barclay Townsite (the original spelling for Barkley Sound) was the brainchild of the Barclay Sound Land & Improvement Company which incorporated, with a capital stock of $100,000, in February, 1892. The Victoria-based firm proposed to "build. . .up. . .the new town of Barclay, situated on Uchucklerit (sic) Inlet. . . The harbour is three miles long and three-quarters of a mile wide, perfectly land-locked, and a natural harbor. The townsite is admirably situated on a gentle slope from the water. . . ."

To encourage industries to establish at Barclay, on the southern shore of, and midway up, Uchucklesit Inlet, the company agreed to devote 50 per cent of all receipts from the sales of two-thirds of the townsite to improvement purposes. Not only that, but they intended to promote a railway from Barclay to Comox, 50 miles due north, on the east side of Vancouver Island. A preliminary study, they said, had shown that such a railway would "cause all the coal (from Cumberland) to be shipped from Barclay (rather than Union Bay), towage being avoided, as it (is) 110 miles nearer San Francisco (the major market for Dunsmuir coal)." As well, the Barclay Sound Land & Improvement Company would encourage the development of the natural resources of the district, which, they said, were many and would "be a leading factor in building up the new town." (The developers neglected to mention that adjoining Henderson Lake has one of the highest annual rainfalls — almost 300 inches — in North America.)

A plan of the proposed townsite shows that only two streets were named, Railway and Broadway (the former parallelled the shore and undoubtedly expressed the promoters' confidence in a railway to Comox), the rest being numbered.

An advertisement for the townsite heralds Vancouver Island as "the most fortunate in natural resources of any part of America," and listed the resources by which residents of Barclay could expect to benefit: coal, iron, silver, gold, quicksilver and tin; the finest timber; the richest coalfields; the fisheries of the Pacific; the most delightful(!) climate.

On the whole of Vancouver Island, of course, the ideal location was the "NEW TOWN OF BARCLAY, situated at the head of Barclay Sound, on the finest harbor on the Pacific Coast. No towage or inland insurance. The natural terminus for the coming transcontinental line (the long-awaited final link with Vancouver Island). The harbor recommended to the Imperial Government for the naval station and dry dock. (One cannot help but wonder who made this recommendation; Esquimalt had been the naval station from the beginning and was the natural location for a dry dock.) It is the centre of a fine lumbering district. . .PRICES YET AT A NOMINAL FIGURE."

Despite their healthy budget the principals of Barclay Sound Land & Development Company could not convince the world that Uchucklesit Inlet was the site of a future metropolis and, without so much as a whimper, their hopes for Barclay Townsite died. Ever so briefly, just before the turn of the century, it appeared that their immodest claims for the area would come true. In 1897 it was reported that "a general rush has set in in that locality." The following year the Forfarshire Mines Company had high hopes for its Mountain Treasure group of claims, on neighbouring Henderson Lake. Four years later the Southern Cross properties, across the inlet, had an "excellent showing" of copper, gold and silver ore. In 1904 it was the turn of Cascade Copper Mining Company to invest heavily in the development of their iron and copper claims.

Alas, initial indications of high-grade ores failed to produce and the Uchucklesit Inlet mines were forgotten. With them into limbo went Barclay. ♣

SECHART, near the entrance to Pipestem Inlet, owed its brief existence to the Victoria Whaling Company. In 1905 Capt. Sprott Balcom, his brother Capt. Reuben Balcom, and Capt. William Grant began whaling operations with the steamers *St. Lawrence* and *Orion.*

First to practise whaling in the Pacific Northwest were the Nootka Indians of Vancouver Island's west coast, in frail cedar canoes that were dwarfed by the mighty creatures they stalked. The original whaling base in British Columbia was the settlement of Whaletown on Cortes Island, established in 1869, although whaling on an organized basis had begun the previous year. Within three years, despite a promising start, the expanded British Columbia Whaling Company passed into history.

It was not until 1905, with the formation of the Victoria Whaling Company, that the industry was revived. Over the ensuing years the original organization bore the names Canadian Northern Fisheries, Pacific Whaling Company and Consolidated Whaling Corporation. Whaling stations were established on the west coast of Vancouver Island, at Cachelot (Kyuquot) and Sechart, and in the Queen Charlotte Islands, at Rose and Naden harbours. As had been the case of the British Columbia Whaling Company, the Victoria firm did well initially, its annual income often exceeding $1 million. But, in almost 40 years of operation, the annual catch dropped from 1,200 whales to the hopeless total of 163 in 1942. The fact that Japan, once the biggest customer for whale products, was then at war sealed the company's doom; Consolidated Whaling joined its predecessor in oblivion.

Sechart had long predeceased the company that built it. Originally whales were captured off Vancouver Island, but too efficient hunting soon accounted for these and the whalers,

most of whom had been imported from Norway, shifted operations to the more fertile waters of the Queen Charlotte Islands. For a time Sechart served as a reduction plant.

One of the few reminders today of the old whaling station is a 20-page booklet, published by the Victoria Whaling Company. Entitled *Whale Meat As Food,* it contains 20 "delicious whale meat recipes; tried and true." Among these mouthwatering recipes is that for *Sechart Salad* — 3 cups cold roast whale, chopped coarsely; ⅔-1 cup cooked green peas, 4 radishes (sliced). Moisten with salad dressing, mix lightly with a silver fork, serve on a crisp lettuce leaf, and garnish with slices of hard-boiled egg or tomatoes.

☆   ☆   ☆

Even before the Victoria Whaling Company became interested in Sechart as the site of a whaling station, the immediate area had been the scene of a small-scale mining boom; copper, iron, gold and quicksilver (mercury) having attracted considerable attention from 1895 onward. Initial hopes did not materialize, however, and it was 1927 before Mercury Mines Limited, of Victoria, operated the Sechart, Sechart No. 2 and Sechart No. 3 claims, half a mile from the beach and a mile from the whaling station. A quarter of a century earlier three tunnels and a 40-foot shaft had been driven here, prompted by showings of cinnabar for a width of almost 40 feet.

In his 1927 report to the provincial minister of mines a government inspector wrote: "It is claimed that this and the Kamloops showings are the only showings of cinnabar, not only in the Province, but in the British Empire, the main world supply coming principally from Spain and Italy."

About 1919 samples taken from the old ore dump had assayed .38 per cent mercury, "which was, of course, too low

Capt. William Grant.

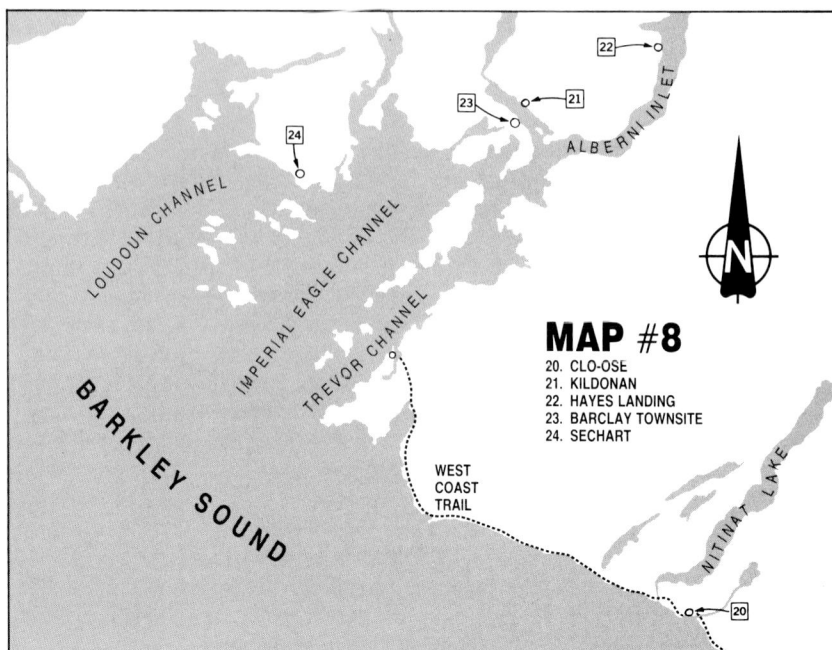

MAP #8

20. CLO-OSE
21. KILDONAN
22. HAYES LANDING
23. BARCLAY TOWNSITE
24. SECHART

(Above left) A Sechart Indian.
(Above right) The old whaling station at Sechart.
(Below) Men flensing a whale at Bamfield c1910.

grade to work at that time. The present price of mercury in Canada (1927) is about $1.25 a pound, giving a value of $9.50 a ton to the old dump." As a result a new company became interested in the deposit.

With government assistance Canadian Quicksilver Company repaired the trail to the mine-site and built a comfortable camp on the beach. Its owners hoped to push the old shaft a further 60 feet but ran out of money. However, manager J. Boss remained optimistic, stating that "with the new type rotary furnace quicksilver can be produced profitably on the

(site) from an ore carrying 3 lb. of mercury to the ton. The present market price is $121 for a 76-lb. flask.

"Samples from the old dump of the shaft average about 0.4 per cent, or 8 lb. of quicksilver to the ton of ore. The property would seem to have considerable merit and, as there is no quicksilver produced in the British Empire, deserves sufficient support to prove it one way or the other."

The "proof" seems to be in the fact that Pipestem Inlet's mercury mine has not been developed into a paying proposition to this day. ♣

Heritage House Publishing Company Ltd.
#108 – 17665 66A Avenue
Surrey, BC V3S 2A7
www.heritagehouse.ca

Library and Archives Canada Cataloguing in Publication
Paterson, T.W. (Thomas William), 1943-
    Ghost towns and mining camps of Vancouver Island

Includes index.
ISBN 13: 978-1-895811-80-3
ISBN 10: 1-895811-80-5

1. Ghost towns—British Columbia—Vancouver Island—History. 2. Mining camps—British Columbia—Vancouver Island—History. 3. Vancouver Island (B.C.)—History, Local.
I. Basque, Garnet. II. Title
FC3844.7.G6P38 1999   971.1'12   C99-910167-6   F1089.V3P38 1999

Cover design: Frances Hunter. Front cover painting: Bill Maximick. Back cover painting: Paul Grignon.
Interior design, layout and maps: Garnet Basque. Typesetting: Kirkrod Printing, Vancouver.

Photo Credits
Provincial Archives of B.C.: pp. 3, 4, 6, 7, 8 (top right), 12 (top), 19 (bottom left & right), 22 (top left), 23, 25, 27, 28 (top), 34, 36 (top & centre), 37 (top), 40 (top), 41 (top left), 42, 43, 45, 48, 50 (top), 51 (top & centre left), 53, 60, 63 (all except bottom right), 65, 67, 75, 77 (main), 82, 84 (all except bottom left), 86, 88 (top right), 89 (top left & right), 90, 91, 92, 93 (bottom inset), 97, 99, 100 & 101 (top right & left).
Hudson's Bay Archives: p. 5.
Sunfire Archives: pp. 9 (top & bottom), 11, 12 (bottom), 19 (top left & right), 20, 21, 22 (all except top left), 24, 26, 28 (bottom), 29, 30, 31, 33 (top left & right), 36 (bottom left & right), 37 (bottom), 39, 44 (top), 50 (bottom), 51 (centre right & bottom left & right), 54 (inset), 55 (top left & right), 59, 61, 68, 73 (top left), 74, 76, 77 (top & bottom insets), 80, 81, 83.
Eric Jamieson: pp. 9 (all except bottom right), 69 (top right inset), 72 (top left), 73 (top right), 93 (top inset).
B.C. Government: pp. 13, 16 (top & centre), 41 (top right), 44 (centre & bottom), 62, 63 (bottom right), 69 (main & top left inset), 72 (top right & bottom), 73 (bottom left & right), 84 (bottom left), 85, 88 (bottom), 89 (bottom), 93 (main), 96 (top).
Vancouver Public Library: pp. 16 (bottom, 46, 88 (top left), 101 (bottom).
Paul Grignon: Paintings pp. 33 (bottom), 40 (bottom), 41 (bottom).
Bill Maximick: Paintings pp. 55 (bottom), 96 (bottom).
Cumberland Museum: pp. 54 (main), 58 (top).

Printed in China through Colorcraft Ltd., Hong Kong

Heritage House acknowledges the financial support for its publishing program from the Government of Canada through the Book Publishing Industry Development Program (BPIDP), Canada Council for the Arts, and the British Columbia Arts Council.

The Canada Council | Le Conseil des Arts
for the Arts | du Canada

BRITISH COLUMBIA
ARTS COUNCIL
Supported by the Province of British Columbia

Index